TENSIONS AND CHANGE

TENSIONS AND CHANGE

The Problems of Religious Orders Today

Gérard Huyghe
Bishop of Arras

Translated by Sister Marie Florette, S.C.H.

74201

THE NEWMAN PRESS
WESTMINSTER, MARYLAND
1966

Originally published, 1960, by Les Éditions du Cerf, Paris,
as *Équilibre et adaptation*

© translation, 1965, Geoffrey Chapman Ltd.

First American printing 1966

Nihil obstat: R. D. Dermitius Fogarty, D.D., L.C.L., *Censor deputatus.*
Imprimatur: H. Gibney, *Vicarius Generalis.*
Datum Southwarci, die 18a Augusti 1965.

Library of Congress Catalog Card Number 65-25983

Made and printed in U.S.A.

This book is set in 12-pt. Linotype Georgian, cast on 14-pt.

Contents

III. FORMATION OF SUPERIORS IN THE EXERCISE OF AUTHORITY

IV. HARD WORK OR EVANGELIZATION?

Translator's Foreword

THE TRANSLATION into English of Mgr Huyghe's *Équilibre et adaptation* presented a number of difficulties because of the documentary character of the original work. In attempting to solve these difficulties with due authorization I made certain changes of which the reader will want to be informed.

The author's documentation is of two kinds. Some facts and figures are quoted merely as local examples and would have little interest for an English-speaking reader; these have usually been omitted. Where there are several omissions of this kind the fact has been indicated in a footnote. Other facts quoted by Mgr Huyghe are either of international interest, or are particularly significant as examples; the greater number are of the latter sort and have been translated in full. When in doubt I have included rather more than less. In some cases general terms have been substituted for specific names of French movements or organizations little known among Anglo-Saxon religious; for example, I have referred to the U.N.C.A.H.S. (*Union Nationale des Congrégations d'Action Hospitalière et Sociale*) as 'an association of religious devoted to nursing and social service'.

The author's colloquial, lively and spontaneous style offers certain difficulties in translation. The present text attempts to find the corresponding English idiom, without sacrificing the spontaneity altogether or, it is hoped, changing the meaning at all.

I take this opportunity of expressing appreciation to my religious superiors, without whose cooperation this translation would not have been possible; to Sister Agnes Gertrude for her patience in reading the English manuscript, and her valuable suggestions; and to Sister Louise Marie for her many hours of service in typing the final copy.

Sister Marie Florette, S.C.H.,
Mount Saint Vincent College,
Halifax, Canada

Preface

Saint Francis de Sales, who was fond of metaphorical expressions, used to compare what he called 'the teachings of devotion' to a bouquet of pleasant and varied flowers. We could use the same comparison for the religious families spread throughout the Christian world. We see them in their various habits, kneeling in adoration night and day before the altar; tending the sick in hospitals, clinics, houses of the poor; enriching the mind and heart of youth; teaching catechism in home or foreign missions, ready even to shed their blood. Hundreds of congregations are thus living and working according to their rule and special traditions. Although they are distinct from each other, a common ideal unites them: the same faith in Christ the Saviour, the same fidelity to the Holy Spirit, the same unfailing love. Down the centuries they have continued, all impelled by the same fervour. But some have sought, besides, to follow the evolution of ideas. They have penetrated to the very heart of those to whom they were sent; they have guessed their thoughts and the tendencies of their soul. They have gradually come to realize that in order to understand their times, they themselves must change. Others, too respectful of their customs, sometimes afraid of being unfaithful to their origins, have perhaps yielded to the weakness of attachment to useless practices. By this very fact they have forfeited the favour of

ix

that youth from whose ranks mystical and charitable vocations are recruited. A further study of the situation discloses
either a certain ineffectiveness and misunderstanding, or
weariness and withdrawal.

The moment has come for all religious families to make
an examination of conscience. Why does not our congregation exercise the same effective influence as in former days?
Why have we not been sufficiently alert in adapting ourselves to our times? Could we not respond more fully to the
tremendous needs which can be satisfied only by renouncing
certain customs, certain habits which have no real ascetical
or apostolic value?

This book is an answer to these questions and this anxiety.
It originated at the meetings and discussions which took
place at the regional congress of religious devoted to nursing
and social service in Lille in May, 1959. It makes a study of
the present and throws much light on the future. It takes
cognizance of the Christian renewal now being effected in
many spheres, and shows the ideal towards which we must
tend wholeheartedly.

I give my blessing to all those who have collaborated with
me in this work of renewal, and to its readers. But above all
I ask God that these pages may cause religious communities
to reflect and to answer this call, which comes to them from
holy Church.

✠ Achille, Cardinal Liénart,
Bishop of Lille

Introduction

IN PREPARATION for the 1959 regional congress of religious devoted to nursing and social service held at Lille, the committee of religious in charge sent the following questions to the Orders and Congregations concerned:

1. What are the essential values of the religious state?
2. Do you think that these values are safeguarded at the present time in your apostolic life?
3. What obstacles do you encounter?

The replies that were submitted, many of them compiled by superiors after discussion with the sisters, contain a wealth of information and instruction.

The speakers at the congress utilized this material in preparing their conferences, and the present writer in particular made it the substance of his own talk which, by its unexpected character, was of help to many uneasy consciences, and disturbed some that were too much at ease.[1]

There resulted many conversations and an abundant correspondence with superiors, sisters, and priests in charge of religious. Gradually the main lines of the present work began to emerge. I shall briefly outline the method followed.

[1] Chapters 3 and 4 of Part I constitute a development of this conference.

The book is based exclusively on the information gathered from the replies submitted by the sisters, and from these a selection has been made. Only those were used which came either from the superiors themselves, or from communities in conjunction with superiors, or from sisters writing under the guidance of their superiors.

Facts are mentioned only in so far as they are relevant; those of an exceptional or doubtful character have been discarded. No abusive generalizations were accepted, nor were examples utilized unless they applied in several cases. In this work I have been actuated by a profound esteem and love for the consecrated life, as well as by an awareness of the sisters' desire to serve the Church, a desire made manifest in the course of retreats and conferences.

I was strongly supported in my work by the priests and religious to whom the manuscript was submitted as it began to take shape. Several major superiors, deeply conscious of the present needs of the Church, contributed their experience and encouragement. To all these I extend my thanks and give the credit that is due.

Far from claiming to have all the solutions, I can barely discern what they are at this time; and if I presume to suggest a few, my hope is simply to prepare the way for a dialogue. Moreover, these solutions are already being applied in some places, and daily experience has also taught me something about the misgivings that I venture to mention here and the hopes that I have for the future.

But my misgivings persist; and since time is not on the sisters' side I must speak out and assume my responsibilities.

Perhaps it will be pointed out that what I say of sisters could be applied to priests, and so it could. The clergy encounter the same problems about recruitment, training, and effectiveness in the apostolate, especially as they are much more individualistic, and their way of life provides neither the organization nor the guidance available to religious. But this book is about the sisters, though if any reader likes to translate it to the masculine, he will not be far from the truth.

For the reader the more easily to follow the method adopted, I shall comment briefly on the sequence of the chapters.

Part I, 'Heirs of the Past or Apostles of the Present?', outlines some of the problems encountered by religious. Both the past and the present are ambivalent. The past contributes the wealth and solidity of spiritual tradition, that is, of the Church, onto which the Congregations are grafted. But it also brings the weight of usages and customs and the immobilism of persons. If tradition is strength, traditions are often a cause of paralysis.

The present, too, is pregnant with promises and dangers. It brings with it new situations, new means of culture and of human and spiritual activity. There is imminent danger of contamination by the sin which at every age the father of lies sows in the field of the divine husbandman. But there is an urgent duty to preach the Gospel afresh to every new generation. The choice is difficult, or rather, there is no choice for an active religious: she must at one and the same time live in the world in order to save it, and be protected from it in order not to be lost herself. To accept today's world and bring to it the message of salvation, she must lean on the best of religious tradition without allowing herself to become rigidly fixed in certain accidental or passing habits which have no reference to the Gospel.

The four chapters of Part I treat of a few aspects of this problem.

The first describes the concern caused by certain congregations which are anchored in the past and seem unable to rejuvenate themselves with the Church.

The second presents the other panel of the diptych, namely the hope offered by other institutes eager to respond to the Church's expectation.

Chapter III, 'Must We Die at Our Work?', raises the problem of the nervous strain of religious sisters whose energy is divided among a multiplicity of apostolic tasks which demand an ever greater degree of specialization. Are they in danger of sacrificing not only their health, but their spiritual life as well?

Finally, the fourth chapter, 'In the World yet not of the World', treats of the permanent choice set before the religious between separation for God's sake alone from a world of sin, and active presence in this same world in order to save it.

Part II, 'An Inner Cloister', details the solution already suggested in Part I. The religious must adapt her spiritual life to the ever increasing demands of the apostolate. How can this be done? Should new regulations be made in order to strengthen the protective structure of her convent life? Should she not rather be freed psychologically and affectively for her to be able to enjoy spiritual liberty, and thus be endowed with an inner dynamism that will protect her more effectively than the most carefully planned environment.

Since this liberation requires a long period of time, perhaps even a lifetime, the formation of the religious must be the task, not only of a novice mistress, but also of the local superiors. True, the opportunities of the noviceship must be fully utilized according to the intentions of the Church; but it is also necessary to bridge the gap that exists between this stage of formation and the rest of life. For the sister's entire life must become a continual formation, aided by the experience and the support of superiors. Such is, in brief, the content of Chapter I.

The three following chapters show how this formation can be given. They develop only three aspects: prayer and the life of prayer (Chapter II); fraternal charity (Chapter III); understanding the cross (Chapter IV).

Other approaches were possible, particularly from the standpoint of the vows. How does the religious life provide a continual formation in obedience, not only of execution, but of inner surrender? How can it teach virginity of heart? How can it be a continual education in poverty, not merely with regard to material goods,[1] but especially to spiritual poverty?

It is not the object of this work, however, to present a treatise on the spiritual life for the use of religious. My aim is different; it is outlined in this introduction and will be repeated in the conclusion.

Since the religious state is a continual formation of the person consecrated to God, it is important that not only the mistress of novices but also all superiors be prepared to fulfil their role. Part III suggests a plan for the training of superiors.

The last part, 'Hard Work or Evangelization?', purposes to help Congregations in adapting themselves wisely to the apostolic needs of today's Church by rediscovering the apostolic intuition of their founder.

A cursory glance at the table of contents will perhaps give the reader an impression of widely varied subjects. A more careful perusal of the introduction and the conclusion will reveal the link that exists between the various sections of this

[1] At times reduced to the practice of thrift.

work. By reading the whole book it is hoped he will derive a satisfying impression of unity.

This unity is founded on the author's earnest desire to be of service to religious, to their superiors, and to the priests who minister to them. It also has its root in his experience of the problems to which the sisters are seeking the answers.

Conscious of the benefits he has derived from this experience, he wishes to express to these religious his heartfelt gratitude.

G.H.

Lille, 10 March 1960.

I

Heirs of the Past or Apostles of the Present?

For it has seemed good to the Holy Spirit and to us to lay upon you no greater burden than these necessary things.

Acts 15:28

The Church, immutable as she is in her principles and in her essential institutions . . . lives, grows, and adapts herself to the new times and circumstances, in order to be in every age the soul of the world.

Pius XII, 24 April 1957

I

The Burden of the Years

If anyone is a hearer of the word and not a doer, he is like a
man who observes his natural face in a mirror; for he observes
himself and goes away and at once forgets what he was like.
But he who looks into the perfect law, the law of liberty . . .
he shall be blessed in his doing.

James 1:23-5

THE WORLD of today is evolving very rapidly. This accelera-
tion of history may be verified not only in the scientific field
in which the past century witnessed changes more rapid than
ever before, or in the political world in which systems fall
and are replaced with unprecedented rapidity, but also in
those areas of thought in which social and human values are
determined.

The stability of thought and of action which prevailed, for
example, in the seventeenth century, is now a thing of the
past. Our civilization is undergoing a crisis; a new world
founded on technical achievement is taking shape before
our eyes, replacing the former bourgeois civilization in which
religious Congregations had their origins after the French
revolution. In this bourgeois civilization they erected powerful institutions which have taken form and give the impression of being everlasting.

In today's world everybody naturally has a job. The

skilled labourer and the technician are becoming aware of the worth and dignity of the human person. Moreover, the world of today is rapidly being dechristianized under the influence of total and massive materialism.

In this context, what is becoming of religious Congregations? What is their attitude? What changes are taking place in them?

They appear to be adopting one or other of two very strong tendencies which, incidentally, are characteristic of all ecclesiastical institutions. Some have completely accepted this new world along with its dangers and its hopes. Resolutely detached from the sociological milieu in which former generations lived, they are alert to the needs of the people who now expect a new type of evangelization.

Others cling desperately to the earlier forms of religious and apostolic life which, they declare, have stood the test of years; and, in the shelter of their institutions which have become for them a sort of artificial Christianity, they do not see that the world is being formed without them and, unfortunately, without the message of Christ which they should be bringing to it.

Sometimes Congregations as a whole have adopted one of these viewpoints as a matter of policy. More often, however, the cleavage occurs in the same community, separating the religious into two profoundly divergent groups : one clinging to the past, the other accepting the present and open to the future. In reality, this cleavage is a manifestation of the difference between two generations. Yet it is a matter of outlook rather than of age. Some religious, though advanced in age, are surprisingly open and eager to adapt, whereas certain younger sisters have a closed mind on this subject.

That there should be opposition between different generations is a psychological or rather a sociological law; tension is inevitable between antithetical forces—the traditionalists and the moderns, or if you will, the young and the old. But today the situation is more serious, for each generation is conscious of its profound solidarity with a human civilization, and deliberately chooses to be committed to this civilization rather than to the other. From this choice are derived different conceptions of the religious life, divergent scales of value, and consequently differing methods in the apostolate.

We must therefore endeavour to consider the reality of the religious sisterhood as it actually exists, with its wealth of possibilities and its variety of aspects. Our objective study discloses many disquieting symptoms.

There is admittedly a risk in gathering all these symptoms into one chapter; shades of meaning may be lost and the reality obscured because it is incomplete. The reader will kindly overlook these inadequacies when he considers that this chapter is merely an introduction, and that it touches upon matters so complex and an evolution so continuous as to require an entire volume for adequate coverage.

Let us adopt the viewpoint of an observer studying religious communities from the outside, and gradually penetrating into the interior of their life.

The first impression he will derive after several years' acquaintance will be the rapid rise in the average age of the religious in the same community or Congregation. A necessary result of this is the closing of many religious houses.

Other missions, however, continue to exist merely by force of habit. When the canonical visitor returns to an institution after a lapse of several years, he frequently finds that the number of religious has decreased and, very often, apostolic works have increased or developed owing to the population growth.[1] One set of statistics concerning the various communities of a single Congregation discloses a decrease of 30 per cent in the number of sisters engaged in the same works over a period of ten years; yet not a single house of the institute was closed. The Superior General of a large Congregation admitted that most of the houses of her Order now established in the French provinces continue to exist only because of the impetus gained in the past, and are staffed by an elderly and overworked personnel. Should she desire to replace these sisters by younger, healthier subjects, a number of the missions would have to be closed. And if we have enough imagination or daring to foresee the situation twenty years from now, we may conclude that unless there is a complete reversal of trends, half the religious houses of today will no longer exist by 1980.

One other factor not revealed by statistics increases our concern: it is the weakened condition of the sisters' health due to their exhausting labours. This subject will be taken up in Chapter III.

If the observer referred to at the beginning of this section is an ordinary person, how will he know the sisters? He will know them by their habit or rather their habits. What will be his astonishment to see costumes so different and cumbersome, head-dresses so unusual and conspicuous; in a word, habits which, for all that they refuse any compromise with modern styles of dress, are more often than not in rather bad taste. At least they might be adapted to the modern apostolate—but that is another question.

The ordinary observer will also be surprised at the formal demeanour and the carefully measured pace of most of the

[1] The author is here referring to situations existing in France. For this reason, several specific examples originally cited in this chapter are omitted in the English translation. Translator.

religious. If he is middle-aged, he will recall that his great-grandmother walked that way. In fact, the training in religious decorum given in many French novitiates today is the same as that which young ladies of the bourgeoisie received a century ago.[1] Many religious congregations offer the last example of the artificial mannerisms that prevailed among upper middle-class ladies of the nineteenth century. Even the parlours with their waxed floors, their primly covered upholstery, their walls decorated with portraits of ancestors (or of deceased superiors general) recall a bygone civilization.

This uniformly reserved and even solemn demeanour is adopted not only with laymen and the clergy, but even with religious of other Congregations. However, a change is fortunately taking place in this regard, partly as a result of conferences for sisters. Only a few years ago they would avoid contact with other religious and gather round their own superiors. On the evening of such a day one major superior wrote:

> The meetings are going smoothly, but they are too highly organized. The climate in which the sisters ordinarily meet is not friendly enough. They too easily overlook simple means which could lend atmosphere and a measure of human warmth—a meal taken together, or even a cup of tea or coffee. Religious of the same city attend a conference on Saint Paul and the first Christian communities. For an hour they share the same spiritual food in a common room. They abruptly leave this table without exchanging as much as a smile of satisfaction over the 'good meal taken together', nor even a friendly

[1] The reference here is to the religious of France. In other congregations, particularly those of Anglo-Saxon affiliation, the sisters' demeanour is much more natural, though still dignified. (Author's note.)

7

'till we meet again' at the next repast to which they have already been invited. And so it is in the rest of their life.

There is another cause for concern. In the course of a sister's day, how many gestures and highly ritualized 'minor observances' there are for which as much fidelity and obedience are demanded as for the constitutions!

Many Congregations possess a true spirituality, obtained from authentic and traditional sources: St Augustine, St Benedict, St Bernard, St Francis, St Dominic, St John Eudes, St Louis Grignon de Montfort or St Ignatius. And they profit greatly from the ministry of priests of the same Order whenever possible, provided the initial excellence of the original rule is not debased by a multiplicity of secondary customs understandable in the Middle Ages, but useless or harmful today.[1]

But in how many Congregations, especially among those founded in the first half of the nineteenth century, is there not even a skeleton of true spirituality. In its place is an accumulation of various practices of piety endeavouring to pass for true spirituality, devotions bearing the stamp of the period in which they originated, left them as a heritage over the years by a former superior general or a venerable ecclesiastic to whom the congregation has remained attached and whose portrait hangs on the parlour wall among the ancestors.

The manuals of each Congregation describe objectively its

[1] Dare we mention the multiple prayers which have accumulated with succeeding generations, and which run the risk of usurping the place of true prayer by stifling it? In many Congregations, fortunately, the introduction of a form of the Office, recited in the name of the Church, and the renewal of mental prayer have disencumbered the spiritual horarium of all these unwholesome proliferations. However, there is still much to be done.

goal, its spirit, and its apostolic orientation. These pages are very eloquent, for they clearly delineate those communities whose spirituality is genuine and profound. But they reveal also the emptiness and bombast of many others in which an abundance of devotions conceals the absence of authentic spirituality.

A glance at the training received by sisters will also prove edifying for our observer. Of course, in many Congregations a very serious effort is being made to make of the noviceship a school of deep spirituality, without cutting it off from real life. This initial formation is periodically revitalized by means of institutes, tertianship, conferences, etc. These activities will be described in the following chapter. But in many Congregations the noviceship is completely cut off from all that is to follow, and there is never again a real opportunity for the religious to reflect and get her breath. Annual retreats, even those made at the motherhouse, do not offer an adequate solution; one cannot in a few days of retreat rethink one's life and compare the theory acquired in the novitiate with the practical experience of the apostolate. The noviceship of one or two years remains for many religious their only period of spiritual formation; what follows is often mere improvisation.

Finally, if our observer were to travel a little and study the distribution of religious houses in order to compare his findings with the apostolic needs of which he is aware, he would make the following observations.

There appears to be no overall plan, either on the part of a particular Congregation, or within a given diocese. Most Congregations have opened houses more or less at random, according to circumstances or in answer to the more pressing demands of some person of influence. Almost all religious societies have known a period of flux, now followed by the ebbing tide. The time of their prosperity enabled them to take root solidly in their home diocese; that was right. They subsequently expanded into neighbouring dioceses and eventually petitioned the Holy See for papal approbation. That, too, was normal and right.

But sometimes, as a result of purely accidental circumstances, a foundation was made at a considerable distance from the motherhouse. In the case of a large Congregation this is no disadvantage, for between the motherhouse and the most distant establishments there exists as an intermediate bond the province; and the provincial superior is careful, by means of regular visitations, to remove the impression of isolation that local superiors might experience.

But in the case of smaller Congregations, some houses are lost in a veritable solitude which can become tragic when the diocesan administration shows too little concern for the spiritual needs of the religious who contribute the help of their zealous labours.

One result of the present decline is a gradual regrouping of communities around their point of departure. It would be desirable for any large scale closing of houses to be subject to integral planning; this would enable different Congregations engaged in complementary works to replace one another in important undertakings which might otherwise be discontinued.

A closer examination of the situation at diocesan level reveals a striking degree of anarchy in the establishment of religious houses. Naturally they are more numerous in the city than in the country, for it is in the urban melting-pot that dechristianization is most active and that there is the greatest scope for evangelization.

But the fact remains that these foundations have been made with no reference to a general plan. One example will illustrate the point. In the education of girls, different Congregations occupy competing rather than complementary positions. This does not necessarily imply that they rival one another; but in actual practice they lean more willingly in the direction of this type of teaching rather than towards other large sectors in which their activity would be fruitful.

The drawbacks of this general situation are very serious, not only for the apostolic works which lack organic structuring, but especially for the individual religious. Too many small convents of two, three, or four sisters, isolated from their motherhouse, are so tied to a parish and to the parish organization that the religious end up by being dedicated to the least fruitful tasks.[1]

In summarizing at the close of this chapter the reasons for concern which have been collected in these few pages, we are faced with the seriousness of the problem and cannot but deplore it. However, it will now be easier to gather together the many motives of hope to be found in the rapid evolution of certain other Congregations.

[1] Bazaars and school fairs, counting the Sunday collection, laundering of linen, care of the church, etc.

2

Promise for the Future

No one puts new wine into old wine-skins . . . But new wine must be put into fresh wine-skins.

Luke 5: 37-8

SOME SUPERIORS general have been acutely conscious of this dispersion of effort and its resulting ill effects; they have therefore sought to regroup their communities according to the means offered them by present legislation. As Canon Law is rather reticent on this subject and suggests only *extinctive fusion*, in recent years the Sacred Congregation of Religious has opened the way to a greater concentration of energy by encouraging every well-intentioned effort and accepting all possible forms of reorganization.

Extinctive fusion is a drastic procedure. The epithet 'extinctive' is dismal, not to say macabre; and it is understandable that smaller Congregations (and with greater reason, the others) will not hasten enthusiastically toward their juridical death. Extinctive fusion demands that one institute join another in such a way as completely to forfeit its identity in favour of the other. The harshness of the measure obviously does not consist in the manner in which it is carried out, but in the fact that it is not easy to face certain and imminent death. Time passes, the novitiate has been empty for many years, the aged die, the other religious grow old, houses are suppressed one after the other. Once superiors abandon all hope of revival, they look about for another Congregation more alive than their own, which will agree to receive them.

Experience proves that such fusion should not unite two moribund Congregations, for this would only increase their weakness. On the contrary, a small Congregation that appears unlikely to survive should be joined to a stronger one able to furnish the means for the support of the older religious, and instil new vigour into the works of institutes destined to disappear.

It is much to be desired that the smaller Congregation seek fusion very early, while it has still sufficient vitality to support the greater number of the houses established in the days of its prosperity. Every suppression of a religious house interrupts the advanced activity of the Church in one of her apostolic centres. Unfortunately, however, the Congregation seeking union almost always delays too long and eventually brings only institutions to be staffed and the aged to be cared for. The sole advantage accruing to the larger Congregation comes in the form of property and money, which are sometimes considerable.

It would also seem desirable that Congregations intending to unite should be in some way spiritually and apostolically related. Experience proves that here the personal element is more important than questions of principle. Whenever it has been possible for the superiors general to come to know and appreciate each other, fusion becomes easier, even when it entails the sacrifice of a spiritual tradition or of long-established works. This is as it should be; when the heart is willing, the head follows the heart and abandons objections it might have been inclined to raise.

Fusion, then, entails the suppression of one of the two Congregations, and is therefore difficult to accept.

For this reason another form of reorganization has been attempted in the course of the past fifteen years; it is known as *federation*. This procedure has proved successful for monasteries of nuns. Up to this time, these monasteries were completely autonomous, often subject to episcopal jurisdiction. They recruited locally, formed their own novices, and were united with other monasteries of the same tradition and spirituality only by ties of friendship. The Sacred Congregation of Religious strongly encouraged the organization of federations. A religious priest was appointed to establish preliminary contacts in each region. Here again, the psychological preparation is of primary importance and sometimes requires several years; but after this necessary delay, the federation begins to take shape. The monasteries retain their autonomy, but the superiors elect, for a term of three or six years, a federal president aided by councillors. A religious priest appointed by the Sacred Congregation acts as guide and adviser. The federal superior is 'first among equals'. She has no executive power but she may, in her motherly interest, visit the monasteries. During the first years of federation it is recommended that she exercise this prerogative very tactfully. The statutes of the federation are extremely broad and allow exchanges among monasteries. They even make provision for a possible common formation of mistresses of novices, until such time as a common novitiate may be erected. In a word, a federation possesses a definite structure which is more or less flexible according to circumstances. (It is extremely flexible, for instance, in cases where there has been strong and lasting opposition to the federation.) But the structure is there and it is evident that it contains the germ of a centralizing and unifying force.

What has been done for monasteries has been attempted, sometimes with great success, in the case of Congregations.

The forty-six monasteries of Canonesses Regular of St Augustine, a nursing institute, formed a federation in 1946, each house retaining its autonomy. The federation is governed by a superior general who, at present, resides at the house of her profession in Malestroit, Morbihan.

In the diocese of Bruges in Belgium, ten small Congregations formed a federation. Candidates to the religious state spend their postulancy and take the habit in the institute of their choice. Then they make their noviceship together in a house belonging to the federation, under a mistress of novices appointed by the president of the federation. It is an interesting sight to see in one house, within a community so diverse, novices wearing different headgear and receiving the same formation before rejoining their own Congregation.

The formula according to which federations are organized is thus very broad and very flexible. In Australia, one federation even unites active Congregations and contemplative monasteries. Although these institutes are so different, many exchanges take place among them, and these not only in the spiritual order. They bring psychological support by lifting religious houses out of a depressing sensation of isolation, and by imparting to them a sense of belonging to a powerful and closely knit group.

The confidence of those outside the convent corresponds to that of the religious within, and vocations to the sisterhoods are beginning once again to fill the recently depleted novitiates. Moreover, when very different forms of religious life are federated together, possible exchanges permit a redistribution of subjects. By this means those who come to realize after several years that they have been misdirected, are enabled to find a milieu and an apostolate in which their youth is renewed. Most Congregations devoted to the active apostolate have subjects who, at about the age of thirty-five, experience a strong attraction for the contemplative life. And in many monasteries are to be found some who, as they advance in age, resist with difficulty a very strong tendency to introspection; these could attain their equilibrium in a more active apostolate. The rules governing Congregations and monasteries are too rigid to allow experimentation after perpetual or solemn vows. The solution offered by a transfer or exclaustration is at present too difficult; it involves too great a risk, and in case of failure, the return of the religious resembles too often that of the prodigal son, with neither the fatted calf nor the merciful welcome. Within a federation such as that which exists in Australia, on the other hand, the transfer of a religious from an active Congregation to a contemplative monastery or inversely, takes place as it were by osmosis, without embarrassment or harshness.

The formula of federation is thus very flexible and adapted to the most diverse situations. In any case, it involves some structuring under the presidency of a federal superior, and possibly closer juridical bonds as well. For this reason a still more flexible form of organization is being devised at the present time, namely *prefederation*.

In one country[1] there exist a number of autonomous religious communities all following the Rule of St Benedict. Some are true monasteries of nuns with solemn vows and major papal enclosure. Others are simple diocesan Institutes exercising the most diverse forms of apostolate: teaching, nursing, care of the sick in their homes. The history of each house is very different and so are its religious traditions, an element not to be overlooked when regrouping is envisaged. Therefore an attempt is being made to establish only prefederation involving all the advantages of federation—

[1] The name of the country is withheld because this pre-federation is still at the planning stage.

exchange of subjects, spiritual relationship—without the requirements of the formal organization. True, there will be a federal president, but she will be a queen without a crown. The term 'pre-federation' seems to suggest that this stage is transitory and intended to precede federation. It is still uncertain, however, and it is quite possible that this tentative arrangement may last indefinitely.

Between the two extremes of extinctive fusion and pre-federation, there exist many intermediary forms. Only one will be mentioned here, because of its significance and the success with which it has been implemented—that of union. There have been and still are in France several Congregations of teaching Dominicans founded in the nineteenth century. Since they possessed the same spirituality and the same habit—which is important—they conceived the idea of regrouping themselves. Work on the project was begun and went on for several years; the meetings of the superiors general, at first somewhat reserved, gradually became more and more cordial. In 1956, four of these Congregations (a fifth joined them later) accepted the principle of their own disappearance in favour of a new institute which came into being under the name 'Union of St Dominic'. For a period of three years the former Congregations continued to exist *juridically*, but ceased to exist in fact. The Union of St Dominic, on the other hand, existed only *in fact* under the direction of a prioress general elected for the duration of the experiment. But it had not yet a 'moral personality' in the proper sense of the term, and had no true juridical existence. Thus in the event of the experiment's proving a failure, the former Congregations would resume their autonomy, and there would be no break in the continuity of their juridical status. But the experiment succeeded; the five Congregations of Dominicans officially ceased to exist in December 1959, and the Holy See conferred upon the new body the name of 'Roman Congregation of St Dominic'. This solution was brought to a successful conclusion by Fr A. Motte, O.P., and could serve as a model in many situations. True, the former Congregations had to disappear, but none to the disadvantage of any one of the others. Psychologically speaking, this procedure is infinitely more acceptable than extinctive fusion, and more efficacious than federation. The example of the Roman Congregation of St Dominic may inspire the superiors general of a number of Congregations throughout France which share the same spirituality, the same apostolic works, the same name, sometimes even the same habit and the same founder, with only slight differences of a merely local character.

The reorganization of religious sisterhoods has only just begun. We must be alert to the fact that time is passing and that it works against us or rather against the Church by closing down every year more apostolic centres in every part of the country, and often the most deprived. Such regrouping undoubtedly requires patience, skill, even diplomacy; and it is unfortunate that these human precautions must be stressed more than a spirit of faith and an unconditional search for the greater good of the Church.

What is far more comforting is the effort of many Congregations *to adapt* themselves to the needs of the times. This was the theme of many addresses of Pius XII to religious in the course of his pontificate.

At first, some superiors frowned upon the idea. How reconcile fidelity to one's tradition with the principle of adaptation? Most of them soon understood, however, that the concept of tradition may be interpreted in various ways. Tradition is not routine; it is not an iron collar, but a dynamic principle.[1] Pius XII wrote to Cardinal Micara, 12 November 1950, on the occasion of the first international congress of religious:

> In relation to the training of souls consecrated to God and the pursuit of works of the apostolate, what is in fact necessary is so to recreate and renew minds and wills, with the aid of the grace of the Holy Spirit, that as far as possible the new fashions of our time and the spiritual destitution of our age will be met. Complete reform of oneself . . . is not achieved by any means equivalent to the disowning or unreasoning contempt for what has been achieved by the laborious strivings of those who have gone before us, and which should be regarded as the glory and ornament of each one's religious society. Reform means, rather, not to lead a sluggish, idle life . . .; it means striving by every means that the holy laws of one's institute will not appear as a collection of exterior and useless regulations, whose letter, in the absence of the spirit, kills.[2]

In his allocution to the Jesuit Fathers, 10 September 1957, the Pope determined precisely the relation that exists between adaptation and tradition. 'There is no one among you who would criticize or reject innovations . . . merely because they are new. On the contrary, it is . . . the constant tradition among you, to apply yourselves wholeheartedly to any new activities which the good of the Church demands . . and not to shirk any work of "adaptation", as it is called.'[3]

Cardinal Larraona, then secretary of the Sacred Congrega-

---

[1] This subject will be taken up at greater length in Part IV, Chapter III.

[2] Abbé Gaston Courtois, *Les États de Perfection* (Fleurus, Paris), No. 321. *The States of Perfection* (Dublin: Gill and Son, 1961), p. 142.

[3] *Ibid.*, No. 644, p. 299.

tion of Religious, gave an important address (9 December 1957) at the congress of religious at Rome, on the principle and meaning of adaptation.

> The movement for adaptation initiated at the congress of religious in 1950 . . . proposes the individual, collective, and social renovation of the vocation to the life of perfection and to the apostolate; and that at every level—ascetical, disciplinary, formative, administrative, apostolic, cooperative. . . . To adapt oneself is, in the true and practical sense of the term, to accomplish in all things, with the generous and magnanimous spirit of the holy founders—for they were true precursors in their own times —what they would do if they were alive today. From this simple idea issued the principle which enables one to discern what is . . . to be jealously guarded . . . and what, on the contrary . . . may be safely pruned, wisely adapted and completed.[1]

This principle of recourse to the apostolic intuition of the founder had already been set forth by Pius XII at the congress of religious on 8 December 1950, in his famous allocution *Annus Sacer*:

> When young people hear it said: 'We must belong to our time,' 'Our endeavours must be equal to the demands of our time,' they are inflamed with an unwonted ardour of spirit and, if they are serving in the ranks of religious life, it is towards this objective above all that they are eager to direct the strivings of their future religious activity. And indeed that is partly correct. For it has generally happened that the founding fathers of religious institutes conceived their new undertakings as a means of meeting needs or tasks of the Church that were then emerging and brooked no delay; consequently they

[1] Document loaned by the permanent Committee of the Religious of France.

adapted their undertakings to their own time. . . . Act in the same manner as they did. . . . Otherwise you will not be able to enlighten, help, support and guide your contemporaries.[1]

The duty of adaptation applies in every area. Pius XII said to the Brothers of the Christian Schools, 6 May 1951, 'The art of education is, under many aspects, the art of adaptation'.[2] He likewise declared emphatically to the nursing sisters of Italy:

> It is unnecessary for us to re-affirm our conviction of the irreplaceable role of women religious in many fields of the Catholic apostolate; above all in education and the school, no less than in works of charity. The very missionary activity of the Church has been, now for a long time, almost inconceivable without the participation of the sisters. . . . But since you are a body of women consecrated to God, and offered to the Church in the spirit of an abiding holocaust, it is always opportune, indeed sometimes it is necessary, that from time to time the balance-sheet of your activities should be drawn up; on such an occasion there should be an examination of certain ways of life and modes of action, in order to see whether they are still useful and efficacious, as they were in the past.[3]

A great deal has already been done to ensure adaptation in the areas of the religious life, the formation of young subjects, and the apostolate. As a result of general chapters and under the impulse of prudent and daring superiors general, some Congregations—large ones and even very small ones—have implemented changes so radical as to appear revolutionary. Names will not be mentioned, first because my information is incomplete (the institutes are too numerous), and also

[1] Courtois, *op. cit.*, No. 415, pp. 182-3.
[2] *Ibid.*, No. 324, p. 143.
[3] *Ibid.*, No. 622, pp. 286-7.

because certain Congregations are still prisoners of their past. In general, however, religious are more open and better disposed to adapt their apostolate to the needs of the modern world than is the average parish priest; but they are still bound by many accidental ties from which they dare not or cannot free themselves.

In one sphere, however, some rather obvious modifications have been effected, namely, in the religious habit. Pius XII referred to it more than once in his addresses. On 15 September 1951, he said to teaching sisters, 'Select one of such a kind that it will be an expression of religious simplicity and modesty'.[1] The following year, in an allocution to superiors general, he was far more explicit:

> In this crisis of vocations, be watchful lest the customs, the way of life or the asceticism of your religious families should prove a barrier or be a cause of failures. We are speaking of certain usages which, if they had once a certain significance in a different cultural setting, do not possess it nowadays; they are such that a young girl, who is genuinely good and courageous, would find them simply hindrances to her vocation. In our exposition on the subject last year, we gave various examples. To return to the subject and say a word on the question of dress: the religious habit should always express consecration to Christ; that is what everyone expects and desires. For the rest, let the habit be suitable and meet the requirements of hygiene. We could not fail to express our satisfaction when, in the course of the year, we saw that one or other Congregation had already taken practical steps in this regard.[2]

The words of the Pope have already been heeded by many religious Congregations, and here and there a simpler headdress has happily replaced a more complicated structure. The address of Pius XII is unmistakably clear. 'The habit

[1] *Ibid.*, No. 445, p. 198.   [2] *Ibid.*, No. 478, p. 216.

of a religious should be expressive of her consecration to Christ.' And he adds, not without a touch of humour, 'For the rest, let the habit be suitable and meet the requirements of hygiene.' Perhaps more remains to be done in this regard, for reforms have been brought to bear on the head-dress rather than on the length of material used for the habit. But the impetus has been given and superiors are anxious to express the poverty to which their sisters are vowed by simplifying their religious habit; this will eventually entail a saving which can hardly be estimated. The poor—the real poor—cannot but gain by it. St Vincent de Paul used to say to the postulants of the Daughters of Charity, 'We live at a time when no unnecessary expense must be incurred. Public destitution surrounds us on all sides. . . . We must have compassion on those who suffer it.'

In addition to the movement toward adaptation, considerable effort is being exerted by many Congregations to give the religious a correct *scale of values*. The idea may appear somewhat obvious; but it expresses clearly one of the points on which Pius XII insisted most strongly, as well as the direction in which religious have most resolutely committed themselves in the past fifteen years. This subject will not be enlarged upon here; for the object of the present volume is precisely to demonstrate what has been accomplished in this regard, and to accentuate what has been so well begun.

1. *Spiritual values*

The Holy Father has often insisted on the importance of the interior life to religious sisters. Their consecration to God demands it and it is this consecration that justifies their existence, for most of the apostolic activities entrusted to them (teaching, social service, care of the sick) could be performed by professional women.

And since they are vowed to the apostolate, they will be mindful that all evangelical work is a 'revelation' of God, an encounter in which those under their care, in the person of the sister, meet Christ living in the Church. But how can an apostle reveal what he has not first discovered himself?[1]

We must not forget, moreover, that evangelical work presupposes a thorough knowledge of the milieu which is to be evangelized, and that this knowledge demands the renunciation of some part of the protection formerly afforded by enclosure. Every apostle today—priest, religious or layman —must therefore carry within himself his own cloister, that inner strength which will not only protect him, but will render his apostolate dynamic and effective.

2. *Professional values*

Every modern religious must be fully competent in the area of her apostolate. Good will and generosity are no longer sufficient; she must possess the human qualities and professional skills demanded of lay experts. The most diverse orientations of the apostolate are now the object of scientific research. There is an art of teaching children how to pray, of cultivating their natural virtues, of fostering in them a living faith. And this art cannot be acquired without a knowledge of psychology and pedagogy.

The care of the sick likewise requires medical competence and the acquisition of the necessary professional qualifications. Social service urgently demands not only a knowledge of laws, but especially a knowledge of people and the art of getting them to reveal their true needs.[2]

The religious of today must therefore study, undergo

[1] This subject will be discussed more fully in Part IV, Chapter I.
[2] It will be sufficient to cite here (since it is unfortunately impossible to do more), the value of psychological training founded on case-work.

examinations, attend conferences; in a word, she must be willing to make an investment of her time.

3. *Intellectual values*

This professional formation is necessarily specialized. A sister cannot be competent in all spheres. It is absolutely necessary to be competent in a special field, and this demands such concentrated effort, that there is danger of narrowing one's horizon and restricting the intellect. For this reason the specialist needs the support of a broad intellectual formation.

Thus a religious will learn to see beyond her own narrow sphere. She will come to discover spontaneously what is positive and worthwhile in all whom she meets, even those who seem most hostile, taciturn, or inept. She will become able to lead them to the discovery of their positive worth, their hidden and hitherto unsuspected possibilities. A narrow-minded priest or religious with negative views ought never to engage in the apostolate. This does not mean that everything, error as well as truth, is to be accepted without distinction; error must be recognized for what it is. But the judgement need not always be made known. The best is so often mingled with the worst that love for the human person and openness of heart are often the best means of eventually bringing the other to distinguish right from wrong and to rectify his position.

This breadth of understanding does not consist merely in openness to persons; it also includes openness to all other forms of the Church's apostolate. While the religious concentrates on one field, she must at the same time broaden her horizon to the dimensions of the Church. Let her then be guided by a Church ever youthful, ever evangelical, ever growing, and let her be full of sympathy and admiration for what others are doing outside her own sphere of activity.

Thus she will be full of courage to work and die in the small, lowly sector of action assigned to her by obedience.

Progress in this direction has been remarkable of late years. Instead of being plunged into an apostolate for which they are not prepared, the newly-professed are now frequently sent to study. Superiors general have been willing to invest a time-fund and devote several years to a serious doctrinal formation and an intensive professional training. In some Congregations the young sisters are not sent out permanently on apostolic work before their perpetual vows. This gives them five and even six years of spiritual, doctrinal, and professional preparation before they are sent on their first assignment, where they will exercise an apostolate for which they are fully capable because of their aptitudes and diplomas. The results of this course of action have already begun to make themselves felt.

All these advantages are to a large extent the result of a new sense of *collaboration* among religious of different Congregations, as well as among religious, clergy, and the active laity.

Collaboration among religious has been made possible by the creation of unions formed according to the apostolic specialization of their members. The two congresses of religious in 1950 and especially in 1957 gave institutional and juridical form to these unions. There are unions of religious devoted to teaching, to nursing, and to social service; as a support for the whole structure, the union of major superiors has acquired, by its very existence, a juridical personality, and has been officially recognized as having pontifical status. The existence of these unions is by now well established in France, and its advantages for the apostolate are already becoming evident.

Pius XII said at the first international congress of teaching sisters held at Rome, 13 September 1951:

> To secure such a favourable outcome, harmony and generous understanding between different religious communities can make a great contribution. Mutual acquaintance and encouragement, a saintly rivalry, cannot fail to prove advantageous to all. An excellent beginning has already been made; you have only, therefore, to continue to advance.[1]

Indeed, and apart from unions, collaboration among religious must become habitual even at the local level; thus haphazard activity will be avoided and the apostolate more intelligently carried out.

Collaboration with the clergy is also facilitated at the present time by an increased openness of religious to the apostolate of the Church.[2] True, there are still some Congregations that seem to exclude the priest from their works, but they are becoming rarer.

In an audience with religious devoted to apostolic works in the Italian parishes, Pius XII declared, 5 January 1958:

> Although it is the priest's responsibility to provide wholesome and prudent spiritual direction for girls, he needs the collaboration of the sisters who, being intimately acquainted with young people, are able to assist, support, and comfort them. The Church depends a great deal on them as the specific instruments which the priest must use in the formation of girls.

Religious are also showing greater willingness to cooperate with the laity; and what is more important, they are now

---

[1] Courtois, *op. cit.*, No. 453, p. 201.

[2] Cf. 'Le rôle du prêtre dans la formation des religieuses à l'apostolat', *Le rôle de la religieuse dans l'Église* (Paris: Editions du Cerf, 1960), pp. 185-202.

increasingly accepted by active laymen as full-time collaborators. However, much ground still remains to be covered in this area. The subject will be taken up again in the last chapter of this work.

Finally, this cooperative activity of sisters of different Congregations, of sisters and priests, or of sisters and laymen, will be carried out under the authority of the bishop.

Pius XII has often reminded us that the bishop has sole responsibility for the apostolate in the territory under his care. He coordinates the activity of all those who labour in his diocese. Hence the increasing importance of those local committees of religious who, under the direction of a central advisory board for apostolic works, distribute the diocesan assignments to the sisters in their specialized fields.

There is indeed reason for tremendous optimism with regard to the future, a greater optimism than the concern voiced in Chapter I would seem to indicate. But the concern is there, and it might be well to give it our attention as we express the hope that soon it will no longer disturb those who believe in the greatness of religious consecration, and in the irreplaceable mission of the sisters in the apostolate of the Church.

3
Must We Die at Our Work?

The body is . . . for the Lord, and the Lord for the body.
And God raised the Lord and will also raise us up by his power.
Do you not know that your bodies are members of Christ? . . .
Do you not know that your body is a temple of the Holy
Spirit within you, which you have from God? . . . So glorify
God in your body.

1 Cor. 6: 13-20

THE QUESTION posed by the title of this chapter must not be
answered too readily by a yes or a no. What is important is
not so much to die as to do the divine will, whether this will
leads to the life or the death of the body. The saying, Ask
for nothing and refuse nothing, has been attributed to St
Francis de Sales or St Vincent de Paul; but the sense of it
must be clearly understood. If it is necessary to refuse
nothing, it is to God that such an offering must be made, and
it is his will that must be obeyed. Why would this will necessarily lead us to exhausting weariness, declining health, illness, and even death? The worst of it is that following such
a programme, souls are in danger of dying before bodies;
and the death of souls is as efficacious as the death of bodies
in wiping out Congregations.

The facts are numerous and distressing. One sister, theatre
sister in a hospital, did not have a single normal night's sleep

29

for three weeks, and was unable to take part in any community exercise. Another sister writes:

> Twenty-five years of obedience have provided a hard and rich experience. . . . One of the most serious flaws in our apostolic life is overwork, which unsettles a person both humanly and spiritually. . . . Our life is not one of service but of bondage. Since we can no longer dominate our work, we have become slaves to it. What should have proved a source of daily spiritual strength has become a cause of daily dying.

In a primary school, three sisters are not only in charge of the administration, but personally teach a total of 120 pupils. On the morning of their free day they conduct catechism classes; in the afternoon, youth club meetings; Saturday night, sacristy duty; Sunday, supervision of the children at church, and youth clubs. Then there is the June bazaar, and when vacation time comes, summer school and youth clubs.

I. CAUSES OF OVERWORK

Three causes are discernible: present-day external conditions; the interior complicity of subjects; insufficient organization of the work by competent authority.

1. *Present-day external conditions*

For a religious member of an active Congregation, there is much more work today than formerly. The sick were as numerous then as now, but they were not given as much medical attention; care of the sick whether in hospitals or at home was much simpler. The attractiveness of technical progress will be mentioned later; but the burden it places on active religious should be stressed here. There are not sufficient lay helpers, and when there are enough, they are on duty only during regular hours of work. Tasks to be done after hours or on Sundays devolve upon the religious who are always on call. All take a vacation except the sisters, for holidays bring extra work in the form of highway accidents and emergency cases, and the religious are always there.

The responsibilities of sisters nursing the sick in their homes are increasingly heavy; children are more numerous and housing developments are rapidly increasing, while the number of sisters is decreasing.

Teaching sisters have many more students than formerly. A religious teacher who had twenty-five or thirty pupils a few years ago, now has forty-five. We shall not mention the overcrowded conditions of kindergarten and primary classes, and their wearing effect on the sisters in charge of them. Such examples could be multiplied indefinitely; one has only to look around.

The duties of sisters engaged in parish work are also much more complex than formerly, when these were limited to Sodality meetings and word-for-word catechism recitations. New forms of apostolate have now been added; there are (thank God) new techniques employed in Catholic Action and catechetics. Yet for all these tasks, there are no more sisters than before. Times for rest have vanished, and if a religious should obtain some respite in her employment, she would hesitate to make use of it while her sisters are working against time.

2. *Interior complicity of subjects*

Among the causes of overwork, not the least is an innate eagerness for desperately hard work. Besides, certain religious consider a multiplicity of duties a sign of generosity. 'We are pleased,' they write, 'when we have managed to crowd many tasks in a single day.' The nature of this activity sometimes betrays itself by the sisters' unwillingness to let others help, under pretext that the work will not be well done. One community writes, 'We are not sufficiently concerned with essentials. We give too much attention to subordinate matters which, with a little organization, could be entrusted to others'. Thus they allow themselves to be wholly possessed by the work begun, and want to finish it at all costs. In the end the work becomes, not that of a religious, but merely of a professional nurse or housekeeper.

Besides, it is more difficult for a woman to get a total view of things and organize her tasks according to a hierarchy of values. She lacks a certain depth of vision. Within her field of consciousness, everything appears equally important. And when urgent demands are made upon her, they carry more weight than the truly important ones. This distinction between the urgent and the important is not merely a play on words; it deserves the greatest attention. How many lives —and here we refer to men as well as women and to priests as well as religious—are so encumbered that the *important* obligations, those which are essential in the mind of the Church, the certain and permanent expression of the will of God on the execution of which his judgement will bear— these obligations are obscured and obliterated by the sheer abundance and proliferation of *urgent* tasks. This is where the complicity of subjects manifests itself. *Important* duties are often exacting; they require sustained attention and great perseverance, and usually do not bring the natural satisfaction associated with the accomplishment of urgent tasks which produce immediate results. One person cannot do everything, and much courage is needed to establish a hierarchy of values, do the most important, and put the rest aside.

Our age is mad on statistics. Results must be tabulated, and always show an upward curve; reports of achievement must be compiled for the admiration of civil or religious authorities. Output and productivity are words used not only in the sphere of economics. It is very gratifying to be able to inform higher superiors and the diocesan or municipal authorities that every year more patients have been visited, and more pupils are in regular attendance at school. All this is human, and would not be tragic if the race for results did not terminate in physical and spiritual exhaustion. Fatigue brings on more fatigue; after a time one becomes the victim of a veritable intoxication which is analogous to drug addiction. One becomes incapable of pausing in the midst of work, and this is the clinical symptom of a nervous system dominated by fatigue. Should rest or a reduction of work be suggested, the opposition comes not so much from superiors as from the sisters themselves. Activism has become so much a part of them that when they are compelled to pause a moment and take stock, they hardly know what to do with themselves.

3. *Insufficient organization of the work by competent authority*

The fact of having to direct an undertaking and render an account of it to higher superiors frequently results in local superiors giving more attention to the success of the work than to the welfare and development of the persons engaged in it. There is a permanent and insidious temptation to use persons merely as means.

A case in point is the present overpopulation of the classroom. It has been proved that in a class of more than thirty students, personal and efficient contact of the teacher with her pupils is no longer possible. But of late years the thirty has become thirty-five, forty-five, fifty. Why not engage lay teachers? Because either they are not available or they cannot be paid, which is probably true. What is the superior to do in such a case? Accept the increased numbers with a word of encouragement for the teaching sister, or refuse children beyond a certain number and incur the reproaches of the pastor and the parishioners? It cannot be denied that this is a distressing problem for the superior who has to solve it. Human beings are at stake. There is no doubt that in the present case her duty is to refuse; but great courage and even heroism is required to do so, for she must face the reproaches of the pastor and often of the best parishioners.

Priests should consider the religious working in their parish as their choicest collaborators, and they themselves should see to it that a proper balance is maintained in their religious life. Yet some pastors are responsible for the over-loaded assignments of the sisters. Often the priests entrust all the material tasks of the parish to them. That a sister should be in charge of the vestments and their repair may be allowed; she may even be sacristan in cases of absolute necessity. But for her to do the work of laymen by taking charge of the material organization of bazaars and outings is today contrary to the dictates of common sense.

II. RESULTS OF OVERWORK

Here the answers to the questionnaire spoke volumes; beneath impersonal phrases could be discerned a hidden anguish.

1. The first thing to suffer is *prayer*. No doubt the superior will see to it that the sisters are present at their spiritual exercises, but while the body is in the chapel, what is there in the heart? It is a purely physical presence; the spirit is completely empty and incapable of concentration. Too many problems have to be met and physical fatigue is almost overwhelming. There is no alternative but automatism and sleep.

In spite of the liturgical renewal of our times, certain Con-

34

gregations still recite the complete rosary for their only divine Office. The rosary has the power very rapidly to lead to contemplation a fervent religious whose life is well balanced. But there is no prayer that so easily becomes mechanical when fatigue prevents concentration and control of the imagination. A programme of prayer thus ritualized is simply an added burden and becomes odious. How can such prayer be spiritually efficacious? Is true interior prayer possible under such circumstances? Our Lord taught that vocal prayer is worth only as much as its interior content (cf. Matt. 5).

Everywhere the pattern is repeated: 'There isn't time.' The capital importance of prayer will be considered later under the topic of the influence of the spirit of the world on the religious life. Nervous fatigue compromises the normal exercise of prayer. Not only is the time given to prayer shortened, but that inner sanctuary which should be free for a disinterested encounter with God becomes invaded by the imagination. All agree that interior recollection is becoming increasingly difficult.

'Beware of the agitated and worrisome activity which allows neither the time nor the calmness in which to listen to Jesus,' said Pius XII to the nursing sisters of Italy, 24 April 1957.

The very grave danger incurred by overburdened religious must be emphasized. Their life has meaning only if it tends to continual intimacy with Jesus. They can be happy only on this condition. If their work exhausts them to such a degree that moments assigned to prayer are moments of sleep or moments of emptiness when they are not moments of unbearable enervation which they endeavour to shorten by any means in their power, the sources of happiness run the risk of being permanently dried up—that happiness proper to the religious life, legitimately aspired to on entrance into the novitiate and nourished by genuine prayer.

2. After the taste for prayer, it is the *power of reflection* that is harmed. The sister can no longer remain alone with herself. Even if she had time, she has not the power. The stress of life continually calls for relaxation and for an unwholesome exteriorization.

The result is that she does not reflect sufficiently on the apostolate itself, on the milieu in which she works. She isolates individuals from their environment; instead of listening to them she imposes her own views. She applies ready-made solutions to all cases alike. Far from fostering individual development, such an approach stunts it, for there is no longer any respect for the human person.

3. *Chastity* is endangered by excessive fatigue.

When a religious works beyond her strength, her hours of sleep diminish in quality as well as in quantity. As a result there are periods in the day when her will is dormant, while her imagination is alert and external activity is multiplied. Lack of sleep produces a dissociation of the faculties; the memory and imagination are always active (hence the possibility of dreams) but the will is inert for the greater part of twenty-four hours. This slumber of the will explains how a person is less vigilant against the phantasms of an overexcited imagination, or the introspective tendencies of an unbalanced sensitivity.

4. Fatigue atrophies *the witness of charity*.

A sister absorbed in her own work is unable to share with others, or become interested in the apostolate of the Church or even of the community.[1] Although she still associates with

[1] Throughout this work the word 'community' is used to refer to the members of one religious house rather than to an entire Congregation. Translator.

her sisters, for example at recreation (which is one of the most important aspects of community life), she has not the strength to react against instinctive individualism, or care enough about others to listen to them with attentiveness and concern. One community writes:

> Each one looks after her own concerns. The tendency is to safeguard jealously for herself these moments of respite, to the detriment of her availability and openness to others and her sympathetic attention to their interests.

In a word, fatigue destroys unity of minds and hearts and leaves persons merely working in juxtaposition. Such a situation also has repercussions in the area of chastity, for isolated activity results in isolation of the heart. When a community is nothing more than an agglomeration of unrelated individuals, each is left without strength or support in the face of discouragement or introversion consequent upon difficulties or a possibility of failure.

The children, the sick, or even the other religious may become the victims of her nervous tension and irritability caused by fatigue. But why let herself go so far? Certainly, she is obliged to love those with whom and for whom she works; only on this condition can she become a revelation of God to them. But she must have the nervous strength to do it.

Some even go so far as to confide their personal or community difficulties to their patients or to lay collaborators. Then the witness of charity is not merely absent; the contrary witness is unfortunately given. The unhappy compulsion to seek a confidante and talk of oneself closes the heart against listening to others and leaves one inattentive to deeper realities.

Religious will perhaps say, 'If we were more numerous, we

should not be so tired.' Let them ask themselves why they are not more numerous; they will find that one of the most frequent causes of the decrease in vocations is overwork. Sincere girls with genuine vocations turn away disillusioned and repelled from Congregations obviously devoted to activism.

The disquieting phenomenon of decreasing vocations gives cause for serious reflection. It has been remarked that the shortage of vocations is evident especially among nursing and teaching sisters, the two categories most likely to be overburdened. To bewail the absence of a spirit of faith in Christian families or of a spirit of sacrifice in modern youth will not solve the problem. Though these causes certainly exist, religious Congregations are not without their responsibility in the matter; for insufficient recruitment is derived in large measure from their incapacity to solve the problem of overwork.

III. SOLUTIONS TO THE PROBLEM

Yet to say that the die is cast and nothing can be done is surely a pessimistic view which cannot be justified. Before seeking remedies, we should look carefully at the life of the sisters. They themselves have furnished the facts and ideas which form the substance of these pages; this work is therefore their own in a special way.

Many religious are restless and uneasy; they have the impression of being crushed beneath a problem which is all the more insoluble because it is vague and mysterious. Their replies were eloquent in pointing out the dangers of activism, but neither superiors nor sisters were very forceful in suggesting solutions. Let us be daring enough to do so on their behalf by facing the reality of the problem in all its dimensions.

One profound cause of overwork lies in a kind of contempt

for the body, the result of a false notion of asceticism and of the nature of man. The body is not the enemy of the soul but its companion, saved by the bruised and risen Body of Christ. It deserves respect. But if in their hectic lives religious despise it, it will no longer be capable of fulfilling its providential role as companion and servant of the soul; it will hinder its spiritual flight.

What actually happens at present? Religious accept all the work that presents itself, all activities, all changes. With the day thus completely filled, they try to snatch a few moments of difficult prayer. As to repose for the body and legitimate relaxation for the mind, they have not the time, the strength, or the permission to be concerned about that. They would feel rather guilty about it. So they act like poor architects who economize on the foundation of a house, and overload the upper storeys.

Let us rather build the house according to the plan of God. The *foundation*, which must be solid, is a sound body; the *first floor* is the life of the baptized soul, the child of God; the *upper storeys* represent the apostolic life.

1. We shall begin with *the foundation—the body and good health.*

The first evil, the most insidious and the most serious, is lack of sufficient sleep. Without a normal amount of sleep it is impossible, absolutely impossible for a religious not only to maintain herself in good health, but also to make the effort to pray and to hold her soul in her hands at the time of work. Lack of sleep dissociates the faculties and completely sterilizes the will. If religious refuse to face this problem seriously, it is vain to ask the questions which are the object of this work. There remains only to await the spiritual atrophy of persons, the growing poverty of health and the dying out of Congregations. It must not be forgotten that the hours of sleep allowed by ancient custom no longer suffice for the youth of today. Moreover, the rhythm of life has shifted at least three hours during the past century; people retire later and do not rise as early as formerly. Young sisters may with difficulty learn to retire at nine o'clock, but they will never learn to rise at the hour the older sisters did. Obviously they can be compelled to be present at early spiritual exercises; the body is malleable enough for that. But the spirit does not follow and it is not until after breakfast or later that it emerges from the fog which surrounded it at dawn. At this moment, however, three hours of the day have already passed, the three most important hours, for that is the time devoted to prayer in which the religious should find the joy of a heart consecrated to God.

To sufficient sleep must be added each day a time of relaxation and recreation. I shall return to this subject presently.

Every religious should have a weekly day of rest which will be for her the Lord's day. In theory, Sunday is the Lord's day for the entire Church; but work is often unavoidable on Sunday. Besides, it is usually impossible for all the members of a community to be off duty at the same time. The superior should therefore assign the work in such a manner as to give each sister a free half-day with the corresponding night. The night must be long enough to enable the religious to make up lost hours of sleep.[1]

What will they do during these hours of rest? Here we must not hesitate to be radical. Let them do as they

[1] Each sister should have her private room. After a heavy day's work she will rest better and relax more completely if she can escape the promiscuity of a dormitory, which adds a useless burden to the trials of common life. Some will say, 'What about asceticism and the spirit of penance?' The present day requires of religious another type of penance. We must not indiscriminately term 'penance' what is merely the customs of another age.

please—true rest and relaxation are to be found in this freedom. If they wish to sleep, let them sleep; if they wish to pray, pray—and they will surely experience a desire to pray. Should they prefer to read, sew, or go outdoors, let them peacefully do so with the blessing of their superior. If, for psychological reasons, it is difficult for a sister to relax in the environment in which she habitually works, let her go to a neighbouring house, even of a different Congregation. This would foster a fraternal exchange which is in line with the friendliness engendered by unions among religious families, one of the most valuable contemporary developments in the religious life.

The opportunity for a sister to employ her time of leisure in whatever manner she wishes deserves special emphasis. According to certain ancient traditions, some religious are as dependent on their superiors as girls in the Middle-Ages or even in the seventeenth and eighteenth centuries were on their parents. But times have changed; and in the best Congregations the training in obedience given during the noviceship leads to a spiritual liberty in which a sister's abiding personal search is for submission to the fatherly will of God. This happy evolution could find expression in the external customs of the institute. Some will express surprise at allowing so much freedom to the religious. Will they not waste their time and be exposed to dangerous temptations? Superiors who periodically allow subjects to do as they please have understood that they are dealing with adults, or at least with religious called to become so. They have understood that training in the use of freedom is truly according to holy obedience interpreted in the light of the Gospel. They have accepted the risks involved in such an experiment. Is any true education possible without risks? Let it not be said that such was not the founder's intention. The founders could not foresee everything; they legislated for an age in which the tempo of life was measured and well regulated, Sunday was a day of rest, and there was no problem of overwork.

To a weekly day of rest should be added an annual vacation. Some religious have no other vacation than their yearly retreat during which they sleep a great deal, for which they can hardly be blamed.

It may be objected that in a hospital, for example, a sister renders such highly specialized service that an annual vacation would not be possible, that the doctors would not allow it. But do not the doctors take a vacation? Let the superiors general of nursing Congregations join in their efforts to negotiate, and if necessary demand of civil and administrative authorities a more humane daily timetable, a weekly day off, and an effective annual vacation for the sisters. It is indeed easier to ignore these problems; but the day is passed when superiors could be content, faced with the gravity of the evil, to raise their arms to heaven and appeal to the faith and spirit of sacrifice of their subjects.

The annual vacation should last one or two weeks, away from the house in which the sisters usually work. In one community of sisters devoted to the care of the sick in private homes, the local superior has arranged, with the approval of her superior general, to have the sisters replaced by secular nurses at a given period each year. At this time the whole community goes by train to a boarding school which the girls have just left. There the sisters rest, read, and restore their physical and mental energy. The two- or three-weeks' vacation period ends with the annual retreat. Then the sisters are prepared to begin the year and resume their work.

Other communities for whom the nature of the apostolate renders it impossible for all the sisters to take their vacation together do so in groups; they have the use of a teaching institute's country house, or the guest house of a contemplative order. Many superiors, then, have not awaited the last warning to take action in this regard.

2. Once the needs of the body have thus been cared for, *the first floor* can be erected.

All the religious must be given time to pray and, what is just as important, time to do some personal spiritual reading as food for prayer. Consecrated religious life is but the full flowering of the grace of baptism, and the purpose of the vows is to cause the grace of divine filiation, the reflexes of a child of God, to penetrate deeply into every detail of life. This is why fidelity to one's 'exercises', while it is a true means of safeguarding a minimum of prayer and a protection against the invasion of work and the temptations of activism, will not alone enable the soul to direct her course towards God in spite of occupations and preoccupations. The interior life of a child of God must besides be nourished by selfless prayer in order later to be nourished by action. Each religious must herself wage her own battle in making a choice on occasion between exacting occupations and prayer or reading rendered more arid by fatigue.

Another fact of experience must be faced. The spiritual timetable proposed to religious by the constitutions, to which they must make every effort to be faithful, daily gives way to the pressure of work and the weakness and weariness of each sister. Now this framework requires daily exercises—meditation,[1] Mass, examens, Office, rosary, spiritual reading

---

[1] The term 'mental prayer', referring to the reality of pure prayer, seems preferable to 'meditation'. But in how many Congregations has not the teaching of pure prayer been omitted and the religious condemned to meditate for ever, no doubt through fear of false mysticism.

in common. This framework comes to us from the monastic life, either of the Benedictines or the Mendicant Orders of the thirteenth century, or of the Brothers of the Common Life (who, moreover, are partly the inventors of methods of meditation).

In a word, the spiritual life has been canonized into a daily schedule which must at all costs be protected against externals. But we must be realistic. This battle is never waged without defeats, especially in modern life. What is sacrificed is the 'unselfish' part of this schedule, personal prayer and personal reading.[1] We usually manage to give the required time to prayer, but we are very conscious of the fact that its quality leaves much to be desired. We must not be too ready to resign ourselves to 'the prayer of stupidity', when we know that something could be done about it.

The necessity and the possibility of authentic prayer force us to insist yet more on the urgency of a more balanced life. Why not have a weekly, rather than a daily time requirement for prayer? By this means, part of the prayer which was impossible on a crowded weekday could be made up during the week-end when religious are both freer and more rested, or during the weekly free day mentioned above. Experience proves that those who avail themselves of this weekly pause not only regain their taste for prayer, but are much better equipped on the following days to resist the corrosion of fatigue and the temptations of activism.

3. Finally, upon these solid and well built foundations *the upper floors* can rest secure.

Religious will perhaps notice that it is necessary to restrict

[1] We suggest that religious be free to make their mental prayer elsewhere than in the chapel, where they are conscious of one another and of irritating proximity. Could they not pray in their rooms? God is not absent from there.

these activities, for it is impossible to add one minute to the twenty-four hours of the day. Superiors will then need much courage to refuse the tasks offered to their communities. They will need more strength to refuse than to accept, for it is more humiliating and always more heart-rending to refuse requests which seem so well justified. But they will say 'no' to excessive work only to say 'yes' to the physical and spiritual equilibrium of their sisters, and they will notice that in the end, the efficiency of the religious is greater not only in quality, but also in quantity.

4

In the World yet not of the World

The creation waits with eager longing for the revealing of the sons of God . . . because the creation itself will be set free from its bondage to decay and obtain the glorious liberty of the children of God. We know that the whole creation has been groaning in travail together until now.

Rom. 8: 19-22

I. TECHNICAL CIVILIZATION AND THE APOSTOLATE OF THE RELIGIOUS

THE EVER growing momentum of technological progress constitutes a new danger to the religious life; but here again, the meaning of this statement must be clearly understood. While calling the attention of religious to the grave dangers of overwork I do not wish to encourage laziness; so I do not intend to promote incompetence by warning them of the effects of technological civilization on the spiritual life and on the quality of their witness to Christ.

In every form of the apostolate the religious of today must be much more personally involved than formerly. All that used to be required of her was to be a religious and possess the qualities natural to a woman: tact and intuition, together with the supernatural virtues of self-forgetfulness and

46

charity. Today the religious must be wholly committed, not only as a woman, but also professionally. In every sphere of activity it is no longer possible to dispense with a professional qualification acquired after serious studies. By assigning young sisters to courses of study, superiors general are showing that they are increasingly convinced—and rightly so—that human competence is not an obstacle to the religious life, but that, on the contrary, it can be the means of giving it a solid foundation. In certain Congregations all the young sisters without exception are assigned to courses of study according to their special abilities; some are trained to become teachers, some nurses or social workers, others are assigned to catechetics, and those whose aptitudes are practical rather than intellectual are trained in the domestic or commercial arts. Thus is avoided the danger of creating a rift between two classes of religious.

Studies do not end with the acquisition of degrees, however, for religious must *keep up to date*. The State devotes increasing attention to this matter, but several organizations of religious sisters have been a step ahead of the State, in their concern to keep abreast of the times and ensure professional competence.

In short, today a religious must be a specialist in her field. Formerly the various members of a community could replace one another, thus lightening the burden of individuals. Today a specialist cannot easily be replaced.

Finally, technical development requires a constant modernizing of the means of action at the service of the apostolate. Many religious drive cars, and it is very well that it should be so. For the classroom, up-to-date textbooks and teaching aids and equipment, as well as adequately stocked libraries, are a necessity.

What are we to think of this technical efficiency? In itself

47

it is indifferent, and belongs to that immense category of human activities which begin to assume a positive moral value only when a specific motive prompts their adoption. Thus by the grace of Christ and the transforming power of charity, technology itself is placed at the service of man and therefore of the Gospel. But because of the weight of sin it can also serve to dehumanize and enslave man.

Professional competence is absolutely necessary in all spheres, whether religious or secular, in which sisters are called to labour. The acquisition of this competence is for them a serious duty, for it makes them acceptable to those for whom they work. The witness to Christ that wins souls is normally prepared and made possible by the esteem which professional competence inspires. But this competence is not an end in itself; it is but a means at the service of charity. Pius XII insisted more than once on the necessity of the professional competence of religious. One community rightly remarks, 'It is possible to be professionally successful without being religiously so; but it is impossible to be religiously competent without being professionally competent as well'.

The Holy See has insisted more than once on the need for thorough competence in religious. In an address at the first international congress of teaching religious, Pius XII said, 13 September 1951 :

> That presupposes that your teaching sisters have a perfect knowledge and command of their subject. Make provision, therefore, to give them a good preparation and formation, which will also meet the qualities and qualifications demanded by the State. Give generously to them all that they need, especially in the matter of books, so that they will be able to follow up afterwards the progress of their subject, and thus give to their young pupils a rich and solid harvest of information. That is in conformity

48

with the Catholic conception, which gleans with gratitude everything that is naturally true, beautiful and good . . . .

Furthermore: the majority of parents entrust their daughters to you for motives of Christian conscience. This, however, should not involve for them the disadvantage of an inferior standard of teaching in your schools. On the contrary, you should make it a point of honour to guarantee for these parents the very best instruction for their daughters, and that even from the elementary schools.

Do not forget either that competence and good teaching win for the sister the respect and consideration of the girls. And then she will be able to exercise a more profound influence on their character and their spiritual life.[1]

In an allocution to the superiors general of women's Institutes and Congregations of pontifical law, 15 September 1952, the Sovereign Pontiff said:

Here there shall be no pettiness; but rather be broad-minded in your outlook. Whether it be a question of education, pedagogy, care of the sick, artistic or other activities, the sister should have this sentiment: mother superior is giving me the opportunity of a formation which will put me on an equal footing with my colleagues in the world. Give them also the possibility and the means of keeping their professional knowledge up to date. . . . We are repeating it in order to stress the importance of this requirement for the peace of soul and the active work of your sisters.[2]

A year before, 31 July 1951, Fr Larraona, Secretary of the Sacred Congregation of Religious, had sent a circular to all superiors general concerning the technical equipment of young women religious:

[1] Courtois, *op. cit.*, No. 449, pp. 199-200.
[2] *Ibid.*, No. 480, pp. 217-18.

Our Sacred Congregation would feel that it was failing in its duty if it did not, moreover, draw your attention at this time to the grave obligation that falls on superiors general of female Congregations who dedicate themselves to education, to prepare their subjects in appropriate fashion, not merely from the point of view of religious formation, but also of technical preparation.

The sublime mission of teacher, to which God our Lord calls the young sister, causes her to enter, with open heart and trusting soul, into the institute which she has freely chosen in the belief that she will find there the milieu in which her vocation will be able to flourish and fructify for the good of souls.

It would be indeed rash to claim that, after the years of the postulancy and novitiate, which were devoted almost exclusively to the personal religious training of the girl, she now can, straightway, without any special preparation, become a teacher; and still less can she be a responsible, capable and conscientious teacher, even for infants merely.

Our Sacred Congregation knows well the difficulties in which superiors general find themselves, in the face of the pressing requests of Ordinaries who, because of their concern for the immediate needs of the Christian people, ask for the opening of new houses and for the assistance of the Congregations for the education of the people.

But, knowing well that the sister who is well prepared will be able, by herself, to accomplish real good among souls, even the youngest of them, the Congregation does not hesitate to recommend emphatically to those superiors to watch, with all possible care, not only the formation of the young sisters, in accordance with the spirit of the institute, but also their pedagogical and technical training; they can be assured that they are thus fulfilling a very strict duty of their delicate task, that they are labouring for the true welfare of their institute, and are making an effective contribution to the apostolate of the Church.[1]

[1] *Ibid.*, No. 480b, p. 218.

In the *motu proprio* approving the pontifical institute *Regina Mundi*, 11 February 1956, Pius XII wrote,

According to the mind of the Church, it is inconceivable and inadmissible that all those who by their religious profession and apostolic vocation devote themselves to social duties and professions, could be or should be thought to be professionally inferior in the performance and discharge of these duties, to those other women who, for motives that are human, however noble, are employed in the world in the same duties or professions.

This applies particularly, and with all the greater reason, to those women religious and virgins consecrated to God who, especially in our own day, are engaged in many different ways in the education, instruction and formation of youth. Their task is an arduous one indeed, not only because of the temperament of the young and the circumstances of the times, but also because of the wider knowledge of science in its manifold forms, of culture and of pedagogy, which has to be acquired in a long course of studies and put to the test of numerous examinations, and because of other similar requirements that are everywhere laid down for teaching.

No one can have any doubt that these women religious who, by vocation, are the teachers and educators of infants, adolescents and young girls—whether they teach in the secondary and higher schools as in most cases, or have charge of girls who are pursuing university studies, even in public academies, or are engaged in the important works of their own institutes, directing or training their own religious—should have a higher training, technical and above all religious, which will be at once solid, well assimilated and complete, taking their special position into consideration.[1]

Finally, Pius XII declared to nursing sisters, 24 April 1957,

[1] *Ibid.*, No. 575 and No. 576, pp. 267-8.

You must not overlook anything that could make you more competent for the direction of nursing establishments and especially for the helping of the sick. For this work, it is not sufficient that you be religious, and even perfect religious; it is necessary too that you should have the indispensable technical knowledge relating to the new methods of treatment, to the new instruments which have to be employed and to the new medicinal remedies which have to be administered.[1]

II. RISKS OF PROFESSIONAL EFFICIENCY TO THE RELIGIOUS LIFE

It is important for religious to be able to discern clearly the risks of professional efficiency.

Efficiency can exert such a fascination upon certain religious that they become wholly absorbed by the professional aspects of their work, and are at a loss when other members of the community exchange views on problems of the apostolate in order to seek in this way, in the light of faith, the plan of God.

All of religious life, in its formation and in its development, is endangered by the fascination exercised by professional and academic proficiency. Several communities mentioned, for example, that the possession of higher degrees gives certain sisters a feeling of superiority over the others. And the sense of inferiority thus engendered in the latter is no less harmful to a profound spiritual life and to the unity which should reign in a community.

According to Pius XI in his apostolic letter *Unigenitus Dei Filius*, dated 19 March 1924:

Learning without virtue is a source of offence and danger rather than of real benefit. It is generally true that those who show overweening pride, because of the learning

[1] *Ibid.*, No. 630, pp. 290-1.

they have acquired, lose the faith and blindly rush head-long to spiritual death. Students, therefore, must take every means to ensure that the virtue of humility, which is necessary indeed for everyone but particularly to be practised by them, is part of their innermost being; let them remember that God alone is supremely wise by his own nature; the learning that a man may acquire, how-ever extensive it may be, is as nothing compared with the things of which he remains ignorant.[1]

It must not be forgotten that the acquisition of human learning, legitimately attractive to an alert intellect, runs the risk of so completely satisfying its aspirations that it ends by superseding awareness of God and apostolic fervour.

Moreover, professional training has become so important that it sometimes takes precedence over religious training. Besides being longer than the latter, it assumes a greater psychological importance because of the examinations which it entails. According to one superior:

The smallest apostolic activity now obviously demands a much more developed professional training. . . . Truly, for the past ten years, a great deal is being required of religious. . . . After their noviceship, most of them are assigned to studies—secular studies, for the most part— and then they have no other care than their examinations in a university or hospital environment. Having obtained their degrees, the young sisters are sent to the missions, eager to begin their active work. Let us be honest; in these assignments, an immense importance is attached to results. . . . It is a good thing when a religious is dis-turbed by this state of affairs, a sign that the best part of her being aspires to more peace, more union with God.

[1] *Ibid.*, No. 164, p. 71.

But the greatest danger is when the religious no longer suffers and the professional task has definitely deadened her need of God and thirst for the salvation of souls.

Finally, the superiors' replies to our questionnaire were unanimous in pointing out the dangers to the spirit of poverty caused by modern technological progress. They deserve to be quoted literally because of their simplicity and conciseness.

> The search for what is most practical and time-saving (and therefore most costly) places us on a standard of living above that of the ordinary people for whom we work. . . .
>
> It is normal that we should procure all that is needed to facilitate apostolic works. But this search for the most highly perfected procedures results in neglect regarding the care of objects at one's disposal and a diminution of concern about the common property. . . .
>
> It is easy to lose one's sense of the value of money (one may have acquired it by working previous to entrance into religion). It is no longer necessary that a sister earn money for herself by personal effort; she merely handles it. Hence an absence of economical management and the consequent waste. . . .
>
> The sisters are affected by our present-day atmosphere of comfort, our refrigerator and washing-machine civilization. Hence a desire—partly legitimate—for what is most convenient, then what is easiest, and finally what is most attractive.

Religious superiors are aware that criteria for the use of money need to be clearly defined.

> What enables the community to save time and facilitates apostolic work is good; what is simply self-seeking is bad.

54

We must admit that in practice it is not easy to discriminate. But nothing is easy and all of the religious life demands a critical vigilance.

Governmental intervention increases the difficulty. Certain categories of religious receive regular salaries and certain institutions receive grants for their work. There follows a material security for the morrow which has little in common with evangelical abandonment to the heavenly Father.

Religious communities are not alone threatened in their spirit of poverty, but each religious in her personal environment must be constantly vigilant against the ever recurring difficulties in this matter. They will receive gifts from grateful patients whom they have cared for, giving rise to temptations of gluttony or private ownership. The management and doctors place medicines and various objects at the sisters' disposal—whence a tendency to utilize these for purposes other than those intended.

It is well to recall in this connection the constant teaching of the Holy See in recent years. On 23 September 1951, His Holiness Pius XII addressed the Discalced Carmelites as follows:

This poverty must be observed strictly at all times, in accordance with the established rules of your institute, whether in the life of the individual or the life of the community. But the manifold works of the apostolate, such as the care of souls, the embellishment of places of worship, the erection of suitable schools and their organization, the foreign missions, the promotion of learning, and also the payment of just wages to servants, all these call for fairly extensive resources; and this must be accepted as normal and above criticism in the changed conditions of the present time. But there should be proportion between activities and material resources, and the quest for resources should be kept within due bounds; if there should be a superfluity of means, it should be used in a spirit of brotherly emulation to relieve needs of every kind; it is not human foresight, which is always uncertain, but trust in the mercy and help of God, and the generous kindness which goes with it, that will ensure genuine success for religious and their undertakings and win for them the esteem of men.[1]

In this spirit one diocesan Congregation gave up all that it had acquired in one generation for the erection of a large parish school.

On 24 April 1957, Pius XII said to the nursing sisters of Italy:

Be careful of the observance of the spirit of poverty, not only individually, but also collectively. We are well aware of the economic requirements of your clinics, which make it their aim, as indeed they are bound, to be equal to what is demanded for a modern hospital; and we know that it is not always easy in such circumstances to remain wholly faithful to the ideal of poverty. Nevertheless, we believe that we should point out to you the danger of easy temptations, from which women religious who assist the sick are not always exempt: we have in mind certain clinics, where it would appear that in the last analysis the standards are not very different from those of a commercial undertaking.[2]

Along with poverty, a certain traditional form of evangelical charity is threatened. It must be recognized that current procedures in hospital administration tend to separate the

[1] *Ibid.*, No. 463, p. 206.
[2] *Ibid.*, No. 628, p. 289.

sister-nurse from the patient. There are not enough religious to take care of all the services, especially the more lowly. The result is that because of the esteem in which religious are held by the management and the doctors, they are placed at the head of departments in which they direct large numbers of nurses and assistant nurses. The latter are the ones who have direct contact with the sick. We can overlook for the moment problems of competence and possible conflicts between department heads and their subordinates. There is no question here of blindly criticizing a form of hospital organization which, on the whole, has proved satisfactory; nor of altering established structures of religious life or suppressing certain forms of nursing apostolate. But a new type of religious Congregation is envisioned whose members would refuse to assume the direction of institutions. The sisters would live in a convent apart from the hospital, thus safeguarding their freedom and their poverty. They would go to the hospital to work as nurses or assistant nurses according to their qualifications and their competence. In this way they would not be deprived of that humble service to the sick which is essential to the vocation of a religious nurse. The problem of the religious habit is secondary and could be solved by various means in different localities. Besides, do not lay nurses wear a uniform?

This project admittedly involves radical change; but considering the eagerness of some Congregations to adapt themselves to present needs, it is not unlikely that it should find a response among them, unless, in this sphere of the modern apostolate as in others, secular institutes should be the answer.[1]

---

[1] There already exists in Milan one secular institute whose members are called Missionaries of the Sick.

III. HOW DOES THE SPIRIT OF THE WORLD INSINUATE ITSELF INTO RELIGIOUS COMMUNITIES?

What is the spirit of the world? We tend to react un-favourably to this expression, for there is danger of its con-cealing a certain refusal to recognize earthly values, a pessimistic withdrawal from temporal realities. Its signifi-cance becomes clear, however, when we understand it in the sense in which our Lord used it when he contrasted the spirit of the world with that which he came to bring. The spirit of the world has always threatened the religious life because it is opposed to the spirit of Christ himself; and for twenty centuries the Church and the world have spoken a different language because they have opposite goals and are actuated by opposite values. This perennial problem is also present in our times; and it is the dangers of the present day, those which we encounter here and now, that we wish to study with critical attention. In this case also, the sisters them-selves have been the first to diagnose and recognize these dangers.

1. In former times religious were protected, almost in spite of themselves or at any rate without giving the matter any particular thought, by a whole set of customs which partly isolated them from the world into which they were brought by their apostolate. They were sheltered by a sort of enclo-sure from which they emerged several hours each day, only to re-enter it promptly once their work was done. Most of them never went out except in pairs.

Today they remain outside their convents for long hours at a time, and the rule of companionship has been largely dispensed with, rightly it would seem, as a hindrance to apostolic contacts.

Within the convent as well as without, the rhythm of life

has greatly accelerated. Lay people themselves are affected; they experience more than formerly the need to get away at times from their habitual surroundings. Such an atmosphere of breathless haste necessarily exercises an influence on the sisters. They continue trying to reconcile the traditional hours of their spiritual exercises with the demands of the apostolate. But as women nowadays are generally employed in work of some kind, the shift system in working, the different times for opening and closing of shops, the tyranny imposed by the need to travel a long distance from their homes, all necessitate a more flexible programme of common life for religious if they are to exercise their apostolate effectively. The only time when working girls are free should not be the hour when the religious must be at a spiritual exercise.

It becomes concretely evident that the unprecedented pace of human living with its increasingly hectic rhythm exerts pressure upon the calmer and firmly traditional tenour of religious life.

Pius XII called the attention of teaching sisters to this problem in an address, 13 September 1951 :

It is possible that some points of the timetable, certain prescriptions which are nothing more than simple applications of the rule, certain customs which perhaps correspond with conditions in the past, but at present serve only to complicate the educational task, should be adapted to the new conditions. The major superiors and the general chapter shall take care to proceed conscientiously in this matter, with clear foresight, prudence and courage and, wherever the case calls for it, they shall not fail to submit the proposed changes to the competent ecclesiastical authorities.

You wish to serve the cause of Jesus Christ and his Church in accordance with the needs of the world of today. It would not then be reasonable to persist in usages or forms which impede that service or perhaps even make it impossible.[1]

2. The spirit of the world influences the mentality of the religious even more subtly and dangerously than it does the externals of religious life. Before they entered the convent, very few were so fortunate as to receive any kind of spiritual direction, with the result that they arrive with a whole set of more or less wrong ideas, a total ignorance of self-renunciation, and with all sorts of demands (not all of them unjustified) which their predecessors never thought of making.

3. Obedience especially is more difficult for them than for religious of former times. When a girl entered directly from the home, her mother's authority found its normal sequence in the rule of a superior, whose authority remained absolute and unquestioned. But today, those girls are rare who live quietly at home with their parents. After going through a period of training they assume more or less heavy responsibilities as nurses, social workers, secretaries, and even managers. Their character is deeply affected by this new situation. Some have exercised leadership in the field of Catholic Action or catechetics, as scout leaders or counsellors at summer camps; they are accustomed to carry responsibility and take the initiative, and rather enjoy doing so. One superior general (the type is fortunately dying out) declared that she did not like to see former Catholic Action workers enter her Congregation, for, said she, 'they no longer know how to obey'. At any rate it is certain that obedience is more difficult for young sisters today than formerly, for reasons partly independent of the Congregations themselves. A wind of emancipation is abroad:

[1] Courtois, *op. cit.*, No. 447, pp. 198-9.

We arrive at the convent full of independence, and this is precisely the greatest sacrifice we have to make to the Lord. . . .

We tend to be of the opinion that obedience is an obstacle to the full flowering of the human personality, considered so important at the present time. . . .

The world believes that obedience hinders personality development, and considers religious as immature because of the obligation they are under to submit their actions to the control of authority, and to give an account of them.

Indeed, not all of this attitude should be condemned, for it constitutes an invitation to religious and their superiors to throw off certain forms of subjection and a kind of ritualism which is but the shell of true obedience. Unfortunately, an accurate understanding of this deeper kind of obedience is still not very common; there results a half-heartedness in resisting a spirit of criticism which is a subtle manifestation of the spirit of the world in religion. Religious and their superiors today need more obedience, not less; but obedience of the right kind: a profound search for the fatherly will of God, expressed through the constitutions of their Congregation, the will of legitimate superiors, and the call of persons and circumstances.[1]

Moreover, home training is far less strict today than formerly. Young people have emancipated themselves from the custody of elders, from courtesy and respect; the impertinence of modern youth hardly prepares the future religious for that filial respect for superiors nourished by the spirit of faith, nor for respect for the aged inspired by fraternal charity.

[1] Cf. *infra* Part III, Chap. 3.

4. The spirit of the world also influences the intelligence and the judgement of religious. We have already seen that the apostolate today demands of sisters a far greater involvement than formerly. They enter into intimate relations with individuals and families, often in their homes, and this exercises a profound influence on their mentality as religious. Dialogue with lay people can, by a subtle process difficult to describe, open a door to the spirit of the world in the subconscious mind of sisters. They want to understand people in order to help them. With the best intentions in the world they strive to please, and engage in lengthy conversations. Thus it happens that all unawares, through a sort of human respect, they adopt a freedom of attitude with lay people which they believe will do good. They hear objections which they cannot or dare not refute, in order, they say, not to lose contact. Gradually and imperceptibly, doubts thus insinuate themselves into their heart.

5. It is the whole hierarchy of values which Christ preached during all his public life, condensed in the Beatitudes and consecrated by his apparent failure, which is ceaselessly put in question and overthrown by the spirit of the world. The apostolate does indeed, as we have seen, require a greater competence of the religious, for this competence is the means of achieving a practical efficiency legitimately to be sought after. But whether she will it or no, the fact of constantly placing the emphasis on this efficiency hinders her spiritual poverty and the renunciation of her too human views in order to believe, sometimes painfully, in another type of efficiency—unseen and always mysterious, disconcerting and trying to her faith. One cannot seek human success without being, in spite of oneself, profoundly affected.

She who believes in her own efficiency acts as though she were master of all, places her trust in human elements with all the prudence and common sense of the world; she forgets that it is God who is doing the work, and that she is merely his instrument. . . .

Concern for human development blurs the demands of the Gospel; fear of narrow-mindedness conceals the ruggedness of the cross. . . .

We are so obsessed with efficiency that we find ourselves more or less consciously classifying those we encounter in our work as 'worth troubling with' or 'not worth troubling with'.

Teaching sisters are aware of this tendency. Several factors entail stricter requirements of students, especially at the secondary level—higher standards of education, competition with State institutions or even private institutions of the same nature, the massive increase in student population. It is hardly possible to act otherwise; but this habitual concern for 'quality' eliminates entire categories of those who are 'poor' according to the world, to the benefit of the intellectually gifted ones.

6. Whatever the nature of their apostolate, religious are increasingly involved in civil, administrative, or professional life. They cannot but be influenced by the spirit that reigns there: the value of good recommendations, the usefulness of human enterprise which veils contempt for others and disregards the evangelical values of sincerity and self-forgetfulness. Deceit is never justified even under pretext of good works. To falsify the exact nature of a teacher's qualifications, for example, is inexcusable; and yet it is not an uncommon practice. Conscience is not disturbed because somehow everything seems justified when the good of the Congregation or even of the Church is at stake. It must be said again and again that no genuine supernatural life, no true apostolate can be built except on the solid foundations of the

natural virtues and a pure intention.[1] The spirit of the world
is a spirit of deceit for it is inspired by the 'father of lies'.
We must not tolerate such a spirit of 'putting up a good
front', of 'making a good showing' in ecclesiastical or religious institutions.

7. Must we include in this reversal of values effected by
the world in Christian consciences the absence of profound
convictions on the true place of prayer in an apostolic life?
Can we not see in the readiness with which prayer is sacrificed to duty and the demands of the apostolate, a proof that
its capital importance is not really understood? We have
seen how the life of prayer is hindered by activism. No doubt
the framework of the spiritual exercises will be preserved
with more or less success, but what remains most often at
bottom is fatigue and boredom. Assuredly, the arid difficulties of the prayer of fatigue can be offered as a proof of love.
Assuredly also, staunch fidelity of one's presence at the
exercises is true and meritorious obedience to the will of God.
But it is not normal that prayer be habitually painful, fulfilled only through strength of will. The conception of prayer
underlying this virtuous aridity is falsified by the spirit of
the world. For the spirit of the world admits of a certain
necessity and a certain form of prayer. It admits for example
that mental prayer can be a sort of reservoir of spiritual
strength, and that its effect is felt on a psychological plane.
But if this notion is accurate, then the apostolate is but a
place in which are lost the spiritual forces acquired in mental
prayer. And if this is true, one recoils before the prayer of
darkness and dryness which all those who seek God must
experience several times on their way to him. But the spirit

[1] We distinguish between natural and supernatural virtues to
comply with current terminology. But it is certain that, for a baptized person, all virtues are supernatural.

of the world cannot admit that prayer should be above all an offering in single-minded, selfless homage to the honour of the divine majesty and the divine mercy; and this spirit penetrates more deeply than is generally believed into the mentality of religious. This is why most of them take refuge in meditation, or what is easier still, in the reading of a book of meditations, even in common, with intervals of silence and sleep.

8. There is one last value of religious life which the spirit of the world threatens, namely the virtue of chastity. In the exercise of their apostolate, religious cannot close their eyes and their ears; and through these channels penetrate more or less freely a thousand images that risk corroding the heart. The religious exercises her apostolate immersed in an 'aphrodisiacal civilization', and she must be clearly aware of this in order to rise above the level of habitual temptations.

Nursing sisters sometimes acquire a certain freedom of demeanour or of expression as a result of their contacts with doctors and patients. But there is something more serious.

It is usually impossible not to hear the popular music played today in every home, clinic, and hospital.

> Sisters who nurse in private homes listen for hours at a time to music-hall melodies and love-songs which the people do not even hear, for all they want is a background of noise to save them from their solitude; while the sisters, who are not accustomed to this, take it all in whether they wish it or not.

Though aware of this situation, the community that reported it also suggested a remedy, saying that 'such an atmosphere can provoke by reaction a spontaneous prayer'. It must be admitted, however, that such a 'prayer by reaction' does not eliminate the risk of slow beguilement.

It is impossible for religious not to see the illustrated periodicals piled up at the bedside of the sick. Some are obliged to watch motion pictures, not only in order to accompany their students, but also because modern apostles cannot ignore contemporary means of human culture. The same must be said of television, which is now installed in most working-class homes.

There is no question here of fostering an unhealthy fear of all these means through which the people learn to know the world; but it must be recognized that these sources of culture are not uniformly beneficial, and that they are capable of exerting a far-reaching influence on certain temperaments. Not the least of these questionable effects is a search for compensation in these outlets.

Even the family of a religious can become for her a source of disquiet. Home visits were formerly unknown; today permission is legitimately given to visit the members of one's immediate family under given circumstances. But sometimes an added channel is thus provided for the spirit of the world; for all families are impregnated with it to a greater or less extent.

It is certainly not to be concluded that religious should never visit their families. One major superior observed:

> For mature religious totally dedicated to the Lord, contacts with relatives can be beneficial, provided they are made in accordance with regulations. They afford the religious an opportunity of contact with the everyday realities of the life of the people and of acquiring first-hand knowledge of the problems of the laity from whom they are often so far removed. It would be desirable for sisters to visit their relatives in the spirit of the fourth command-

ment, 'Honour thy father and thy mother', in order to bring them love, joy and peace, not to seek compensation for themselves. Let them be for their loved ones at such times of joyous reunion a witness to the love of the Lord Jesus. The way in which certain religious ignore their families produces quite a contrary effect, especially where faith is weak.

II

An Inner Cloister

I now recall that on days when I was over-burdened with material occupations or when I was about to set out on a journey, she would often repeat this warning: 'Make within your soul an inner cell which you must never leave'.

Blessed Raymond of Capua, *Life of Saint Catherine of Siena*

You must build within yourself a room enclosed on every side into which you may retire and always abide there. Wherever you may go, never leave it. Whatever you look at, see it from within your cell.

Saint Catherine of Siena, *Dialogue on Perfection*

For your monastery, you have the houses of the poor;
   your cell, a rented room;
   your chapel, the parish church;
   your cloister, the streets of the city;
   your enclosure, obedience;
   your grille, the fear of God;
   your veil, holy modesty.

Saint Vincent de Paul, *Conferences*

5

The Burden of the Law or the Freedom of the Children of God?

For freedom Christ has set us free.
Gal. 5:1

THE DANGER is real enough. Religious life is threatened today more than formerly; it is in greater danger in the hearts of consecrated religious than in the institutions; it is in greater danger through the conditions of the apostolate than through the lessening of vocations.

Should rules and restrictions be strengthened? It is obviously not possible to isolate active religious from the modern world by an extra cloister. Let them keep merely what Canon Law requires, and it will be quite enough. It is not even desirable that the material cloister be strengthened by means of new directives or a stricter supervision. The life of religious is sufficiently supervized and it is not by such bonds that modern apostles should be fettered.

Should conferences and spiritual retreats be increased in number? It is remarkable how the initiative in this area is coming from so many different sources: from bishops and priests, from the sisters themselves, or better still, from associations of religious Congregations. It is a proof that there is a real need, and that it is a new situation born of present-day conditions of the apostolate. Is this also an imperfect solution to the problem? Yes, if these periods of intensive recollection are inserted into the sisters' schedule *over and above* their usual heavy obligations, instead of being integrated into the regular timetable. Far from providing an occasion of resting in God's presence and of relaxed prayer, such spiritual activities become merely an added burden and cannot bear fruit because the mind is not at rest. Nor is it a good plan to take advantage of a holiday for this purpose. Why this obsession to save time at any cost? Both spiritual renewal and physical rest are important enough for the one not to be sacrificed to the other.

Days of recollection will be an excellent means as long as they are organized in such a way as not to be weighted down by concern over material work on the one hand, nor infringe upon rest on the other. For seed to bear fruit (and the word of God listened to in preaching or in prayer is a seed) the ground must be prepared and free from the thorns of solicitude about work.

Perhaps it will be objected once again that there is no time, that those who suggest such a plan do not realize the problems involved, that the work is too urgent to be put off, and so on—a familiar refrain which has only one drawback, but a very serious one: it ignores the principles of psychology and the relative importance of the problems in question. Superiors who are really convinced that, today especially, the quality of their sisters' spiritual life is more important than their work, even of the most apostolic nature, find time for truly beneficial and strengthening intervals of recollection. And there are such superiors, as well as those who know that they cannot ignore the physical needs of their sisters while supplying their spiritual needs; and these also find means of procuring hours of true rest and a good vacation for them. But there are also the others!

THE HEART OF THE PROBLEM:
RELIGIOUS LIFE IS A CONTINUAL GROWTH

There must be no fear

We must begin by accepting willingly and gladly the whole reality. Technical and pagan civilization is a fact against which it is vain to protect ourselves by artificial barriers, putting our head under our wing and taking a negative attitude. Formerly the apostolate of the religious was exercised in a Christian world, at least in appearance. Upon leaving the cloister of the convent to enter the world which was her field of activity, the religious could easily remain under the impression that the protection of her cloister accompanied her everywhere. Today this world has been dechristianized, or at least has finally assumed its true appearance; and it exerts a strongly paganizing influence. In order to bring to it the good news of the Gospel, it is necessary to plunge deep into the world and incur the obvious risks of contamination.

Concerning the usual temptations which the world opposes to chastity, there can be no compromise. We are here in a domain in which the deliberate acceptance of objectionable shows or dangerous reading or doubtful conversations leads almost necessarily into sin. For this reason no pretext can justify a certain freedom of attitude—neither the young sister's preparation for life, that is, for the depressing situations she may some day have to encounter; nor her desire to evangelize and to save. Pius XII, in his encyclical *Sacra Virginitas* of 25 March 1954, said clearly:

> Flight and constant vigilance, as the means whereby we are carefully to ward off occasions of sin, have been regarded by saintly men and women of every age as the most effective method of successful combat in this field.

73

But nowadays this opinion does not appear to be held by everyone. There are some who hold that Christians . . . should not be as in former times segregated from the world, as they put it, but present in the world: consequently, they should take the risk and put their chastity to the test, and thus it will be made clear whether or not they have the strength to resist firmly; therefore, they contend, young clerics should see everything in order to become accustomed to view everything calmly and thus to become immune from any and every form of temptation. For this reason they would readily allow young clerics to turn their eyes freely, without any concern for modesty, to whatever is presented to them; to attend motion pictures, even those forbidden by ecclesiastical censors; to read periodicals, even if they are obscene, and to read novels which are on the Index or prohibited by natural law. The reason which they allege for allowing all this, is that these spectacles and publications nowadays constitute the mental fare of the majority of men, and that those who wish to be of assistance to them must be familiar with their way of thought and feeling. It is not difficult to see how mistaken and harmful is this method of educating the clergy and training them to acquire the sanctity which befits their calling: 'He that loveth danger shall perish in it' (Ecclus. 3:27). The admonition of St Augustine is relevant in this connection: 'Do not say that your mind is chaste if your eyes are unchaste, because the eye that is unchaste is the messenger of a heart that is unchaste.'

This very dangerous approach undoubtedly is based on a serious confusion of thought. While Christ said of the Apostles: 'I have sent them into the world' (John 17:18), he had previously said of them: 'They are not of the world, as I am not of the world' (John 17:16), and he prayed to his divine Father in the words: 'I pray not that thou shouldst take them out of the world, but that thou shouldst keep them from evil' (John 17:15).[1]

[1] Courtois, op. cit., No. 537 and No. 538, pp. 245-6.

74

In the domain of chastity there can be no question of becoming so accustomed to evil that one is finally immune against temptation.

Having made this reservation, we must accept the fact that at the present time the world is bathed in an unwholesome atmosphere, and that religious will have to inhale this polluted air in spite of themselves. They will have to plunge deep into this reality, that is, affront the paganizing influence of the modern world. A twofold attitude towards it will be needed. On the one hand, this 'reality', far from weighing down their spiritual vitality, must not only be neutralized, but should become the source of a deeper religious life by promoting a sort of instinctive reaction against evil, set in motion by evil itself. On the other hand 'reality' must be evangelized. If sin existed in a pure state there would be no question of this; but objectively, sin exists in a world in which people are more or less contaminated, sometimes without even being aware of it, and without willing it entirely. 'Father, forgive them, for they know not what they do' (Luke 23:34), said Jesus of those who had deliberately betrayed him. Sin exists, but men do not know that they are steeped in it; it is for this reason they must be sought out in their own environment to be saved and evangelized. It is clear that in order to do so, the religious must accept total commitment. But where will be her protection?

In past years this protection was chiefly exterior; today she must find it much more within. There is indeed no question of eliminating all former safeguards to the religious life. On the contrary, none should definitely be eliminated. But the fact remains just as definitely that the problem will not be solved by making these prescriptions harder. What the religious needs today is not more *having*, but more *being*. She needs a much stronger spiritual formation than formerly,

75

perhaps spread over a longer period of time, so that she may carry within herself her own enclosure.

She needs protection, but this protection will come far more from her fully matured and liberated interior life than from an exterior supervision whose limitations are obvious. And it is not sufficient to speak of protection, even if the principle of this protection lies in the centre of the heart. To this somewhat passive and defensive attitude must be added an active and conquering attitude: must not the modern world be accepted and assumed in order to be evangelized? I shall speak of it later but it is not only with regard to God that 'perfect love casts out fear' (I John 4:18). True love of God and man implies optimism and daring in regard to the world.

How will religious acquire the strength of soul required to live in the midst of the world a life genuinely consecrated, and so conquer the world?

A vocation is a continual growth

We usually have a static notion of vocation. It seems to be a gift totally given, all at one time, which can be either accepted or rejected, kept securely in a safe or lost on the way. One 'has a vocation'. Another 'had' a vocation. All this is very convenient. If this is the meaning of vocation, the fact of having answered the call brings great security, and easily lulls conscience to sleep.

Now we find in the Bible that there are always two elements in a vocation: on the one hand, all is given with a call; and on the other, it must grow in the course of a long lifetime (cf. Jeremiah, Mary, St Paul).

In a vocation (perhaps the word should be 'consecration',

as implying a sense of continuity) one's liberty is continuously being exercised: one is constantly called to choose and prefer God. A consecration is a free dialogue between two persons. It is a free response to a permanent call of the Holy Spirit. This free response is constantly being received by the Church in the persons of legitimate superiors, and this gives it its validity and its authenticity.

God calls a girl to the religious state in the sense that he places in her heart the germ of a vocation to a life of consecration. This vocation is given her only that it may grow unceasingly until her death. The responsibility for this continual growth is entrusted by the Church to mistresses of novices and especially to superiors. Everyone agrees on the necessity of promoting this growth during the noviceship. But for too long a time it was the custom, as soon as the noviceship was completed, to send the religious to various works without concern for the progressive spiritual formation still required. Much more attention is being given to this matter at the present time, especially in large Congregations. The canonical noviceship is extended into a juniorate and the young professed often remain under the direct influence of the motherhouse until perpetual vows. Moreover, intensive sessions are being provided more and more after ten, fifteen, twenty, and even fifty years of religious life, along with prolonged retreats of one, two or three months usually called tertianship. All this is excellent, but it is possible only in large Congregations able to supply the personnel qualified for so delicate a task.

The quality of the germ of vocation must be ensured

It is at the time of entrance into the postulancy that

superiors should be wide awake to the quality and the motivation of the candidate's vocation.

It is not sufficient to reject the world; in addition, Jesus Christ must be chosen and chosen with a very clear notion of what is being given up and of what is being undertaken.

What would have been the candidate's attitude towards marriage if she had not had a religious vocation must be discovered. One who is incapable of genuine human love cannot consecrate herself fully to God. The concept of human love as used here does not refer only to love for one's parents; it also includes the possibility of love for someone of the opposite sex. The Immaculate Virgin Mary herself was called to collaborate in God's work not as a simple maiden, but as a young married woman. True, she remained a virgin; she did not 'know' man in the biblical sense of the word. But she loved the husband God had given her; according to the designs of God she was involved in a person-to-person relationship of love. Only one who would have been capable of the fullness of human love in marriage can engage herself in the religious life with the certainty of finding therein the full flowering of her chastity. A dislike for the male sex is not sufficient motive for entering religion. A girl must be capable of normal human love in order to *prefer* the love of Christ. She does not go to Christ in order to escape someone else, but in order to choose him in preference to every human creature.

Future religious usually think of their 'sacrifice' in terms of what they give up. But remembering the etymological sense of the word (the act of making sacred) let them also ask themselves positive questions: what they are offering, what they are consecrating. For it must be well understood that community life does not promote the affective evolution of the individual—on the contrary. There is a stage of this

78

development that the candidate must have passed through before entering religion.

For this reason it is highly recommended that future religious be examined before entering. This should not be a formal, compulsory examination, for such testing might easily inhibit candidates and so render the examination useless. It should take place under circumstances that at all costs respect the individual's privacy and preserve secrecy concerning personal information disclosed. A commission composed of priests, doctors, psychologists and women psychiatrists could be set up, for example, in each large university centre in order, at determinate times, to examine future candidates who would present themselves *freely* before them. The strictest professional secrecy would be observed, no files would be kept, and only the priest who is president of the commission would communicate with the girl, giving her not only the result of each examination, but a judgement of the whole concerning possible affective impediments and the means of overcoming them. Upon entrance into the convent, she would only be required to testify that she did undergo the examination; the results would not be disclosed.

Proper motivation does not involve merely psychological and affective reasons for entering religion, but spiritual reasons as well. She must really desire to give her life, *in a single profound and homogeneous movement,* to the love of Christ and the service of the Church. One can enter religion to care for the sick or the aged, or to teach; one can even enter for less worthy motives. But unless these motives are eventually transformed, one cannot persevere long in the religious life.

Although psychic and affective motivation must be essentially complete before her entrance, a girl's spiritual

79

motivation may be very incomplete at first. But it can become more definite and more deep-seated in the course of her noviceship and her entire life.

It is necessary to have a very definite ideal from the start. Every religious vocation may be defined by two elements: the absolute choice of God, that is, consecration to his service and his love; and the giving of one's life for the good of souls. The point of departure of a consecrated vocation is often the service of others. But it is only a point of departure, and it is normal that one day, the sooner the better, the candidate to the religious life will be captivated by the love of God, and that this love will be such that the gift of her life to others will appear as the necessary consequence of this one love.

Father Daniélou writes:

> The source of the apostolate is not necessity but the exigency of love. What must arouse the missionary vocation in us is, first of all, not the need of souls to be saved, but love of God which leads us to want him to be known and loved. The authentic missionary call has its origin in the pain we feel because Christ is not known or loved. Now, this exigency of love is more urgent than any necessity could be. Here we have a twofold movement: we desire to bring Christ to souls, and we desire to bring souls to Christ. Too often, we think only of the first: that we must bring Christ to souls. If we go no further than that, there is danger that our missionary call will not be urgent enough, and may run foul of certain objections. But if we also insist on the other aspect: that we want to bring souls to Christ because this is the only efficacious proof of love we can give him (indeed, we can add nothing to his interior glory, but only to his external glory); then, the apostolic spirit, flowing from a love of Christ, takes on an implacable urgency. It is in this love that the great apostles have found their élan towards souls. . . .

In our time, spirituality is often too anthropocentric, oriented too much towards the good of humanity as such. This degrades its most essential religious content, and it ends by being an extension of humanism. It is because we love our fellow men that we want them to have all good things, including the benefits of religion; but the starting point remains human. An authentic missionary spirituality must include this attitude, but above all else, it must have its source in love of God and of Christ. In consequence, it must be perpetually rooted in contemplation, which maintains within us this sense of God.[1]

This evolution must be completed before profession and it is the duty of the mistress of novices to see to it. It must be recognized, however, that such an evolution has not taken place in all religious, and there are many for whom the emphasis is placed on the service and evangelization of others. They do not exclude the love of Jesus, but the mainspring of their activities is not this love of Christ nor filial service of the heavenly Father, but love of others.

Yet it cannot be doubted that no true unification of life is possible without *an accurate spiritual aim*. The love of Jesus, and in him, fundamental obedience to the heavenly Father, is the cornerstone on which alone a coherent spiritual edifice can be built.

Founders of religious Orders did not err when they defined in very strong terms, from the beginning of their disciples' vocation, this high spiritual aim. St Benedict commands them to *'seek God'*; St Ignatius, to *'belong to God in all things'*.

But once the emphasis has been truly and solidly placed on the love of God, the religious must at the same time

[1] Jean Daniélou, *Le Mystère du salut des nations*, pp. 138-9; *The Salvation of the Nations* (Notre Dame: University of Notre Dame Press, 1962), pp. 111-2.

integrate love of others into the motive of her vocation. It is obvious that the one cannot exclude the other. But one day, and the sooner the better, she must find out that she has given her entire life to the love of the heavenly Father in Christ and to the love of the Church, and that these two loves are but one and the same love. Such is the 'spiritual aim' that will be the principle of unity during her whole life. We have preferred the word 'aim' to 'goal'. We do not reach the goal until the end of life (and even after). We never belong totally to God and our weaknesses remind us of it daily. But an accurate aim must be taken as soon as possible, in the first years of the apostolate. Religious are submerged in their work rather through lack of a unifying principle than because of the multiplicity of their tasks.

Means of fostering spiritual growth along the religious life

Superiors must be capable of discerning in their sisters the forms of infantilism which will impede their spiritual progress, their adjustment to their work, or their insertion into the community milieu.

The question becomes more important than ever when it is remembered that at the present time it is no longer possible to transfer religious indiscriminately from one house to another. Tasks have become too highly specialized; projects are initiated, experiments carried out, acquaintances made and people's confidence won. If all these links are suddenly destroyed by a change in personnel, all must be begun over again.

But as one major superior reports, it must also be recognized that 'faced with these new exigencies, most of the sisters are not adult either humanly or spiritually. They become attached, sometimes unconsciously, to the people, to the mission, to their sisters. Change disturbs their life; some even question their vocation, their perpetual vows'.

'There are in our convents many chronic adolescents whose heart and will have never been educated. Having remained at the stage of seeking to be loved, they are never satisfied and manifest their lack of affective maturity by moods, jealousy, stubbornness, an unwholesome need of being understood, excessive attachment to a superior or a sister. Thus they easily form inseparable pairs in communities.'

Until the present time these problems were solved by empirical and surgical means. A retreat at the motherhouse made by the sister in a state of mental anguish would culminate in a drastic and unexpected change. Such methods are rooted in a false conception of detachment, and have never brought to maturity a religious whose affectivity has been retarded.

But while it is now necessary to ensure a certain stability of personnel in order to coordinate the apostolic efforts of all, it is above all important to obtain their psychological and affective growth at any cost, and that no longer by coercive means devoid of mystical significance, but above all by a *positive formation* in which the entire human person progresses as a whole—body, mind, and soul. 'The nature of true religious friendship must be explained and thoroughly understood in connection with the requirements of charity. Local superiors must face their responsibilities about the affective education of their sisters, enlightening their conscience and creating a community atmosphere in which true religious friendship can flourish, and deviations become impossible.'

It would be interesting to make a study of the exterior, palpable signs of retarded affective or psychological development. This is not the place for it; but we can ask a few questions on signs of immaturity in the expression of the spiritual life of a religious.

What is her conception of the heavenly Father, the Father of whom Jesus speaks so often with such respect and love? Is it associated with the image of fatherhood derived from memories of her earthly father?

In the course of retreats certain religious are to be found for whom the concept of a heavenly Father is intolerable because they cannot dissociate it from the remembrance of their own dictatorial and autocratic earthly father, one apparently devoid of human feeling. 'Experience shows that the traces of the paternal image are very difficult to eliminate from the religious dialogue, and that the tendency to "paternalize" God, or to fit him into the human father relationship, is all too easy.'[1] Others remember their father as a weakling, and so for them, the heavenly Father never assumes the consistency of a real Person. Yet God cannot be compared with earthly fathers; he is the Father par excellence, alone and wholly transcendent.

What is her conception of our Lady? She will say that Mary is her mother; but in what sense, and what is implied in the word? Sometimes devotion to Mary is hindered by recollections of certain unpleasant or sentimental relations with one's earthly mother.

Just as God is called Father, so the Blessed Virgin will be called Mother. But here, too, this maternity has nothing to do with an emotional intra-family relationship: it is a theological maternity, mystical in the real sense of this word, and universal.[2]

[1] Abbé Oraison, *Amour et contrainte*, p. 146; *Love or Constraint?* (New York: Paulist Press, 1961), pp. 124-5.
[2] *Ibid.*, p. 130.

This is why devotion to Mary is in no way sentimental, but requires on the contrary the full play of faith.

What is her spiritual scale of values? What is the most important commandment for her, not in theory, but in practice, according to her examination of conscience? Confessors are obviously in a better position than superiors to know the conscience of religious; but certain errors in the relative value of things are externally apparent without the need of confession to bring them to light. For example, are there not religious who seem to live a life of intense prayer, yet whose relations with others are apparently empty of love?

What does the word 'rule' mean to her? A setting for her life which dispenses her from reflection and commitment ('I shall have a superior who will tell me what I am to do'), or an ever mysterious expression of God's fatherly will which one must 'seek' (John 5:30) with love in order that it may become one's food?

What is her conception of holiness, that holiness which she probably desires to attain? Is it a perfection of life achieved by dint of increasingly successful efforts, or rather the joyously accepted conviction of her profound wretchedness which God's mercy continually saves? Our whole spiritual vocabulary needs to be re-examined and modified, and that from the first religious instruction given to small children. For example, when preparing them for first communion, we tell them that their soul must be 'adorned' in order to be 'worthy' of receiving our Lord; they should rather be led to a conviction of their weakness, for they can never be worthy to receive him. This is the pedagogy employed by the Church for her priests, as can be seen by reading the ordinary of the Mass. Holiness, then, is not a contest in which heroes triumph, but an adventure of mercy in which the humble of heart and the little ones are filled.

What can superiors do about spiritual immaturity? Let them begin by eliminating from community life all the customs that maintain the sisters in infantilism. I have before me the directory of a Congregation[1] which is a jumble of notes on the constitutions, rules for religious perfection, regulations for the cook, the portress, etc.; a collection of the prayers of the Congregation, a number of subjects for meditation, etc. The lack of order is not too serious; what is serious is the fact that the constitutions and the regulations for the sewing sister are placed on the same level. How can a religious using such a manual escape the impression that according to her training, everything is equally important, and the perfection of obedience requires her to give the same attention to every prescription?

Let superiors educate their sisters in a correct sense of relative values. 'The Kingdom is more important than hell, grace is more important than sin, Christ is more important than our Lady. This enables one to put each aspect of faith in its place without neglecting any, and without allowing oneself to be led by temperament, intellectual or sentimental involvements, or by a confusing proliferation of devotion.'[2]

Superiors must do the impossible to procure for their religious a sound spiritual formation. Many Congregations (again, I am referring to certain very distressing prayer manuals) have more various devotions than genuine spirituality. A great effort has been made to improve this situation during the past ten years. We know of one diocesan Congregation founded in the last century, which through lack of authentic spiritual sources of its own, based its spirituality on the solid principles of one of the great Orders. The result

[1] It should be noted that this directory was suppressed in 1959.
[2] R. P. Liégé, O.P., *Adultes dans le Christ* (Brussels: Ed. de la Pensée Catholique), p. 25.

has been marvellous; the religious are experiencing a spiritual flowering never seen before and vocations are plentiful.

True spirituality has its centre in Jesus Christ, and both dogmatic and moral theology have no meaning but in Christ. The virtues—humility, obedience and the others—are monstrosities when considered as ends in themselves. How can we know humility except through Jesus who revealed it by living it and continues to live it at the present time in those who try to imitate him.

Let superiors be on the alert to discern in their religious any signs of spiritual or affective immaturity. Let them speak to the sister in question with much tact and patience, in a free and relaxed conversation. This is so delicate a subject that a spirit of intervention or severity would close the soul to any beneficial influence. A person must be very well balanced herself to dare point out to anyone else even slight traces of affective unbalance. And who will presume to say she is fully balanced? But if the superior can gain a hearing, she will render immense service to the sister; for once recognized, the disorder is half cured.

It is especially in the exercise of authority that superiors must give proof of psychological insight. This matter is so important that I have devoted a section of this work to it.

All of the spiritual life must be taught in this perspective. Religious must be capable of living fully in the world not only without being contaminated by it, but they must also be so armed psychologically and spiritually as to christianize it by teaching and especially by living the Gospel. For this a sound religious formation is necessary, not only during the noviceship, but continuously throughout the entire religious life.

It is impossible to exhaust the subject. But we would like to indicate some paths to be opened up at the beginning and followed to the very end of religious life with the same single-mindedness of purpose. Thus in the following chapters we shall try to show that the religious life must be a continual school of prayer, a continual school of fraternal charity and a school of the spirit of faith in the clear-sighted acceptance of the cross of Jesus.

6

A School of Prayer

'Awake, O sleeper, and arise from the dead, and Christ shall
give you light.'

Eph. 5:14

The Spirit helps us in our weakness; for we do not know how
to pray as we ought, but the Spirit himself intercedes for us.

Rom. 8:26

I DO not intend to repeat in this chapter what excellent
treatises have already said on the subject of prayer and the
life of prayer. But I do wish to show that prayer, well taught,
becomes a powerful aid to the religious in building within
her, in the interior of her heart, the spiritual cloister which
will protect her against the spirit of the world. Further,
prayer will enable the religious to penetrate into the heart
of the world and place there that ferment of love which
alone can transform it little by little in a mysterious way,
transcending every concrete experience.

But a few essential principles must be emphasized. *Religious life must be a continual school of prayer and of the life
of prayer. This prayer and this life of prayer are the most
powerful means to purity of heart; they are the crucible of
love in which the evil influences of the world, stirring up
original pride within us, are continually destroyed by fire.*

These are the principles underlying every paragraph in
this chapter. It is hardly necessary to add that everything

89

contained therein has been suggested in answers given by religious or by priests questioned in the course of retreats preached by the author.

I. MEDITATION OR PRAYER

The vocabulary is important, for it reveals already the trend established in the noviceship, and certain errors of method. Sisters frequently say that they make (or do not make) their meditation.

What is a meditation? It is a spiritual exercise of reflection and reasoning on a definite subject or a text, possibly with the help of a book adapted to the subject. At the end of this exercise, one endeavours to make resolutions according to the subject meditated upon.

I said an exercise, therefore a human effort, using various long-tried methods, a technique and a personal contribution. It is understandable that a religious should speak of making 'her' meditation. The possessive indicates the human limits of the exercise.

At the beginning of religious life it is necessary. The postulant knows nothing or almost nothing of the message of Christ and the conditions of the spiritual life. So she feels the need of reflecting, reading, reasoning, making use of the faculties: intelligence, memory, imagination, sensibilities, in order to construct an arsenal of beautiful thoughts, strong convictions, solidly founded decisions.

Methods of meditation are numerous. Meditation books are still more numerous—they fill libraries. They are no longer being republished. The whole current of modern religious thought, and evidently also the call of the Holy Spirit, is drawing souls towards pure prayer. But the books survive and have found refuge in religious communities.

It is not my intention to condemn meditation; it is necessary at the beginning of the religious life, for a more or less protracted period according to the individual. It can be useful at certain periods of life, as a discipline and an ascesis of the intellect, and to get back to the right path. But meditation is not necessarily an encounter with God. It merely leads to the threshold of the encounter.

The alarming part is that in many novitiates nothing but meditation is taught. After that, classes are finished. The young religious can only continue according to this method of prayer without ever being taught to pass on to the next stage.

It seems that certain superiors and mistresses of novices distrust any spiritual endeavour other than meditation. They are heirs to a whole current of thought that began at the end of the seventeenth and in the eighteenth centuries, after the quarrel on Quietism; through fear of false mysticism, all mysticism is distrusted. Even today it is generally believed that contemplation is dangerous, while meditation is safe and leaves room for no illusions: once the train is on the track it will never derail, but neither will it get anywhere.

If the fervent advocates of meditation are questioned concerning the reasons for their opposition to pure prayer, they will manifest an unreasoned and instinctive contempt of all sentimentality, of all feeling, as if the characteristic of prayer were to be sentimental, whereas meditation is intellectual.

If religious go no farther than meditation, they never meet God; they meet only their own intellect while they watch ideas go by. Besides, meditation becomes difficult after a time; the slightest word which hitherto brought forth laborious and fruitful reflections, is drained of its content in an instant. Finding herself short of ideas and with a good deal of time left, fearful of a silence whose value she has not realized, the religious takes refuge in reading a book of meditations in order to feed the empty intellectual faculties. I am acquainted with many communities in which, for a half hour each morning, the monotonous reading of a prefabricated meditation is inflicted on all the religious, who are thus constrained to remain at the same stage of the spiritual life.

At the beginning of this chapter I said that the school of prayer should be continuous. Actually, where such a regular school exists, it is a school of meditation in which, during all the years of an entire life, the same programme is gone over again and again. The serious aspect of this situation is that it is possible for a consecrated soul to be faithful to 'her meditation' every day of her life without making the slightest spiritual progress. The practice of meditation does not demand a continual purification.

That is why after meditation the transition to mental prayer must be taught.

During the time of meditation, God is the one about whom the religious is thinking; he is a 'he', in the third person singular, the object of her reflections. As soon as he becomes a 'you', in the second person singular, one to whom she speaks, the threshold of prayer has been crossed. There is yet indeed a long way to go, a certain number of 'mansions' to be visited, but the essential has been accomplished, for she has just surrendered herself to the penetrating action of the Holy Spirit. During the stage of meditation much activity was going on, but it was chiefly human activity. As soon as she speaks to God, as soon as she treats him as Someone alive with whom she is conversing, this conversation is directed by the Spirit of God, and the Spirit unceasingly comes to the aid of our weakness. He will soon teach the soul to pass beyond mere words; for even when they are uttered in the second person, these invite her to reflect on their meaning, and by this subtle temptation to fall back into the snare of meditation.

It is indeed a temptation to wish to understand the full meaning of the words she addresses to God. Besides, this purely mental effort is vain. Who has ever been able to recite the Lord's Prayer with full awareness of the meaning of all the words? It is before prayer, during the stage of meditation that one must reflect on the meaning of words. At the heart of prayer it is sufficient not to think of words, nor even of someone, but to speak to God or better still to love him. It is necessary to 'disintellectualize' contact with God, reduce it to its simplest element, more or less described in the following expressions: 'Repose in God', 'tending towards him', 'needing him', 'thirsting for him', 'seeking the face of God', 'abandoning one's being to God'. Abba! Father. And beneath all these different expressions we discover the first spark of all prayer, the spark of love. It is beyond all thought; it has no need of the help of the feelings. *It proceeds from the heart*, in the Gospel sense of the word heart. Or rather it proceeds from the heart of God, from the Holy Spirit. 'God's love has been poured into our hearts through the Holy Spirit which has been given to us' (Rom. 5:5).

It is easy to understand that he who has discovered in his heart the spark of love brought forth by the Holy Spirit should begin to speak the language of God. There is, in fact, a language of men which they use in conversing with one another; this language supplies words to meditation and even to vocal prayer. But the words of vocal prayer are a human ash covering a spark of divine fire. The language of men was taught us by our parents. The language of God is taught us by the Holy Spirit. It is he who prompts us to say, 'Abba! Father' (Rom. 8:15; Gal. 4:6) in speaking to God. He is the soul of our intercession; he makes us stretch forth our heart

93

to God, like a little child who cannot yet speak the language of men, but can stretch out his arms towards his father with inarticulate cries.

When the spark of love brought to life by the Holy Spirit is freed of the ash which covers it, it is for him who prays to let it increase in intensity by removing the things which could stifle it. This spark may become a vigil light burning before the Blessed Sacrament, or the flame of a candle, or a fire of joy, or a conflagration. But it all proceeds from the Holy Spirit.

Here we can measure the immense distance that lies between meditation and prayer. In meditation, a great effort is made to build up, assemble ideas, take resolutions. This effort is very good, but it is a human effort. In prayer, a man presents himself before God and remains there in all his weakness, but also with love and an open heart, and it is the Holy Spirit who directs the conversation. It is true that this conversation takes place in the depths of the soul, beyond the realm of clear consciousness, and faith alone tells us that this dialogue is taking place. At the end of the thirty or sixty minutes passed thus in the silence of love, we shall perhaps be under the impression that we have been battling against distractions and even yielding most of the time (we shall speak of distractions presently). But our faith affirms that the Holy Spirit is at work here, and that his action in us is far more important than all the words we might have uttered.

By this means the religious can tend towards *continual prayer*. Prayer, even the holiest, is but a means to the end: a life of prayer. It is to this continual prayer that the Lord invites us when he says that we ought 'always to pray and not lose heart' (Luke 18:1). St Paul also recommends it: 'Pray constantly' (I Thess. 5:17).

Much has been written in recent times on the subject of

the apostolate as food for the life of prayer. What progress over the previous generation which was taught a type of prayer removed from life and threatened by it! We are here at the heart of the problem posed in the preceding chapters. How can religious life be protected against the dangers to which apostolic activity exposes it? It is simply a question of finding the means which will make of this apostolic activity the food of prayer. If the fire of prayer has been properly kindled during the time devoted to it, all that is placed therein during the day will itself also be inflamed. It is not possible to describe in these brief pages how and on what conditions the apostolic activity of the religious will permanently nourish her prayer. Suffice it to emphasize the fact that it is a school in which no one has ever finished learning, and in which teaching methods vary according to persons and circumstances. But the teaching must be done, and that without interruption.

II. WHY DO YOU DAILY PRACTISE MENTAL PRAYER?

Experience proves that the principal reason why modern apostles give up trying to live a life of prayer, and even give up mental prayer altogether, is to be found in a faulty or incomplete motivation in prayer.

Four answers to the above question were given by priests and religious engaged in the work of the apostolate.

1. *'We do not know.'*

Extraordinary as it may seem, this answer occurred frequently in various forms. In reality, these people have no idea of the place of prayer in the spiritual organism. When could they have learned? They consider it to be connected with a mysterious law with a dual rhythm: work during the day, spiritual exercises morning and evening; and included and listed indifferently, under the heading 'exercises' are mental prayer, Mass, the Office (or rosary), the examens, spiritual reading in common, etc. Just as all human existence is divided into two parts: night succeeds day; sleep, work; vacation, teaching; death, life; so prayer (and the other 'exercises') succeed activity.

Note the 'ritualism' which characterizes the day of these religious. The letter has been well taught, and it must be recognized that there is a certain greatness in this daily fidelity to the letter. But where is the spirit?

2. *'Prayer is advantageous to us.'*

Another frequent answer. It is in prayer that we find strength for daily living. Prayer is, as it were, a refuelling station.

These answers are very imperfect and even wrong. In the first place, they make of prayer a sort of reservoir of spiritual strength, of generous thoughts, of acts of love, from which to draw during the day. It gives a wrong idea of the apostolate and even of material work performed under obedience, in that it considers them as impoverishing elements detrimental to the spiritual reserves stored up at the time of prayer. The *apostolate*, on the contrary, *must sustain and nourish prayer*, and it is for this that postulants must be prepared; otherwise their life will be divided into compartments, time for getting and time for spending.

Moreover, to speak thus is to consider prayer as a psychological experience falling within the realm of clear consciousness and not the realm of faith. Clear consciousness has little to do with faith, and an intense psychological experience has no connection with the quality and the depth of prayer.

Those who give this answer help us to understand why so many consecrated souls abandon true prayer to take refuge in meditation, reading, or . . . sleep, when they do not give up such practices altogether, if they can. The most general experience tells us that prayer is often dry, difficult, and trying to our feelings; a period during which we unsuccessfully struggle with a terribly unruly imagination, and which therefore often leaves an impression of failure and loss of time. And yet if we have faith and place ourselves in the spiritual conditions required for true prayer, we know that this impression of failure is not justified and that the dialogue directed by the Holy Spirit takes place at such a depth within our soul that it is impossible for us to have a clear consciousness of it.

3. *'Our prayer is useful to those under our care.'*
One priest declared, 'If I did not make an hour of mental prayer each day, my parishioners would be the ones to lose.' For those who gave the above answer, prayer is the time in which the most intense and most efficacious apostolate is exercised. Being vowed to the apostolate, they are convinced that there is none more efficacious than prayer.

The answer expresses a profound truth, but it is incomplete. Nevertheless, it is true, and it should be brought home to candidates to the priesthood and the religious life.

For indeed, the reason why many abandon prayer is to be found in the conviction that the tasks awaiting them are more urgent than prayer and more efficacious for the salvation of souls. Prayer, especially when it is difficult, gives so much the impression of a waste of time while so many urgent problems are waiting to be attended to. If priests and religious were deeply convinced of the apostolic efficacy of prayer, they would have the courage (the word is exact) and they would find the time to make mental prayer.

All of Christian tradition, rooted in the Gospels, has always given precedence to contemplative prayer over apostolic activity, even the most apparently successful. 'This kind cannot be driven out by anything but prayer' (Mark 9 : 29). 'Mary has chosen the good portion, which shall not be taken away from her' (Luke 10 : 42). The teaching of the Church is constant, and among the pontifical texts of our times it will be sufficient to cite that of Pius XI in the apostolic constitution *Umbratilem* of 8 July 1924:

> It is not hard to understand that a much greater contri-bution to the growth of the Church and the salvation of mankind is made by those who are constantly occupied with the duty of prayer and mortification, than by the workers who till the field of the Lord; for if they did not bring down from heaven an abundant rain of divine graces, the evangelical labourers would gather but a meagre harvest from their toil.[1]

The time we devote to prayer (which often seems a pure waste) reminds us daily that God alone saves and cures souls. The priority of the grace of God over every apostolic activity, even purely spiritual, impresses itself on our stubborn and busy minds only by means of the daily offered holocaust of these thirty or sixty minutes spent in apparent passivity.

This being clearly taught and understood, we may say that neither the first nor even the primary reason for prayer is to be found in the apostolate. What then is the primary motive why we should pray at length? The remaining persons answered the question accurately.

4. *'Prayer is a love-offering to God.'*

Yes, God alone is the first and last justification for prayer. We pray on account of him only, for his love, wholly lost in him and with complete forgetfulness of self. Likewise every moment of the spiritual life and of the apostolate is a love-

[1] Courtois, *op. cit.*, No. 177, p. 78.

offering to God. We do not follow a particular course of action even in the spiritual order for a merely human end, even a very noble one. The good of our soul and the salvation of others are profoundly desirable provided we see clearly that they have value only in relation to the ultimate end. It is thus that Christ acted and lived. His apostolic activity, at times so intense, his love for men proved with so much tact and expressed 'unto the end' by his death on the cross, were so many ever renewed expressions of his love for the Father. And this is the only authentic attitude by which the apostles of today can enable Christ, through his Holy Spirit, to continue in them his work of evangelization.

If we have a right idea of the greatness of the heavenly Father and of his immense love for us, we shall know how to give ourselves to him in prayer for his own sake, without looking for results even in the supernatural order. God is great enough to engage our whole attention, and powerful enough to be trusted with the daily offering of a part of our precious time so easily wasted on other things. Here the example of Jesus can help us since the Gospel frequently shows him in prayer in the evening or the whole night through, or in the morning before dawn (Matt. 14:23; Mark 1:35).

If we have a right idea of God we shall understand that our time belongs so much to him that we must, as it were, lose it for him.

Our prayer must be as gratuitous and selfless as the first three petitions of the Lord's Prayer. We pray, not in order to gather strength, but to offer our strength to God. We pray, not in order to receive, but to give to God, to give without realizing we are giving, to give without joy, if need be, and in the darkness to deliver up our being and our life.

III. WHAT PREVENTS YOU FROM PRAYING?

To this other question often asked in the course of our inquiry, the most frequent answer was: distractions.

It is well to exorcize this phantom, for if it is true that distractions are inseparable from prayer in our human condition, it is no less true that they can be extremely enlightening as to the contents of the 'heart', as well as the deepest orientation of the 'heart'. There are, indeed, innocent and inevitable distractions of which I shall speak at the end of this section, for I really wish to help religious, who truly and sincerely make their mental prayer with a heart turned wholly Godward, to surmount the impression of failure and even the feeling of guilt which the continual flow of distractions creates in them. But there are others who manifest perfectly, to one who can interpret their answers, the subtle obstacle which prevents the impetus of prayer. And because they do not recognize the obstacle and eliminate it courageously by abnegation, many consecrated souls abandon mental prayer or take refuge in a substitute.

Liberty of heart and abnegation

In analysing the problem of distractions, it is necessary to explore the zone in which they originate. Too often it is believed they occur in the imagination; this is so only in the case of innocent distractions. The others, on the contrary, are born in the depths of the 'heart', and their projection into the imagination is but a result of their interior proliferation.

What is this 'heart' of which we have spoken more than once? There is no question here of sentiment, nor of the feelings, as present-day terminology would lead us to believe. The word heart is used here in the scriptural sense. For in deed, the heart is 'at the root of our thoughts and our loves, the most personal, the deepest and most real part of ourselves, where our great thoughts and great decisions originate, where we are alone with our Creator: "Pray to your Father who is in secret" '.[1] Jesus has said, 'Where your treasure is, there will your heart be also' (Matt. 6:21). The heart in us is what God sees: 'Thou who triest the minds and hearts, thou righteous God' (Ps. 7:9). The heart is the principle of the deepest dynamism of the human person, that which becomes attached, which tends towards a goal, which pilots a life and redirects it constantly.

In order to be able to pray, we must ask ourselves to what, or rather *to whom* our heart belongs. If the heart really belongs to our Lord it is free, and prayer is possible; if not, the wings of prayer are cut.

Does our heart really belong to our Lord? We may not answer 'yes' too readily, for we do not come to know ourselves all at once. Under normal conditions, however, self-knowledge grows little by little as we advance obscurely towards the encounter with God.

A free heart is one that seeks the Lord alone without stopping at self, without stopping at *anything* ('*Nada*, nothing', said St John of the Cross). That is what all the great spiritual writers have agreed upon, using various formulas. St Benedict, for example, urges the candidate to the monastic life to 'seek God'. St Ignatius of Loyola has other very categorical formulas: 'One must belong to God in all things', and again this expression so often misunderstood: 'One must become indifferent'—indifferent to everything, that is, save only God.

[1] Chevignard, *La Doctrine spirituelle de l'Évangile* (Paris: Éd. du Cerf), pp. 119-120.

This fundamental question, 'To whom does our heart belong?', must be asked not occasionally but every day, and at any rate at the beginning of every hour of mental prayer. One cannot rest satisfied if the heart belongs three-quarters or nine-tenths to God; for if some hidden corner of the heart is not the Lord's, it is from there that distractions will flow into the imagination.

What should concern us in the spiritual life is not what we have given to God, but what hitherto we have refused him. For it is what we have refused that weighs most heavily upon our prayer and is an obstacle to its fervour.

For this reason self-denial is essential to the success of our prayer. St Ignatius of Loyola used to say of a religious whose spirit of prayer was praised in his presence, 'Say rather that he is a man of great abnegation'. The specific purpose of self-denial is to disengage the heart of all that encumbers it and prevents its impulse towards God. Since the heart is never wholly purified because it is the seat of original self-love, the 'sin' to whose power St Paul recognized that he himself was 'sold' (Rom. 7 : 14), and since we shall carry this selfishness with us even to the grave, self-denial must be continual.

The attention of religious should frequently be directed to the fact that self-denial is a preliminary condition for prayer. I have already said that they must be taught continually about prayer during their entire religious life. It is in the context of self-denial and purification of the heart that this education must be ceaselessly given. Self-denial consists in a continual process of freeing the heart in order that the Lord may occupy the whole space.

Every day, and whenever we are praying during the day (the goal is to 'pray always') we must ask ourselves seriously if our heart really belongs to the Lord. Before ploughing the field of our soul in prayer, we must thrust the ploughshare deep into the soil. This we do by asking at the outset, 'Lord, is my heart entirely thine?' On the answer to this question depends all the rest of our prayer.

Distractions arising from introspection

The word is descriptive; it shows a person absorbed in the consideration of herself and her problems instead of keeping the eyes of her soul fixed on God.

This is a common ailment in the religious life; sensitive persons (and therefore women) are particularly susceptible to it. The slightest wound, either real or imaginary, is grievously felt. Every pause in one's activity, every moment of silence (hence the time of prayer) furnishes an occasion of ruminating[1] over the disappointment. The heart is not free because it is occupied with itself, busy with matters of secondary importance; the morbid rumination of its worries fills the field of its consciousness.

Why do such persons keep turning in on themselves? Because a 'sad' passion has mobilized all the powers of their soul. Let us give a few examples of these passions which absorb the heart and hinder the soul's progress.

1. *Too emotional an attachment to persons.* Freedom of heart certainly does not weaken one's power of loving, one's feeling; nor does it kill fraternal charity. On the contrary, it gives to fraternal charity its true impulse. True love excludes no one, while emotional attachment chooses, classifies, eliminates, and opposes. A too emotional and exclusive attachment to a human creature (a superior, a sister, a relative, etc.)

---

[1] Again, a graphic term. Persons who deliberately 'ruminate' or 'chew over' their difficulties and failures are incapable of mental prayer. It is clear that they need the help of meditation books, unless sleep mercifully comes to their rescue.

clips the wings of prayer. The same may be said of every instinctive antipathy, or envy, or jealousy: all that sterilizes fraternal love surely kills loyalty and the taste for prayer.

2. *A hurt or disappointment received and pondered within,* instead of being united with the sorrow of our Lord. It is here that rancours against legitimate authority, spite, bitterness and sadness engendered by inevitable setbacks in the spiritual life or the apostolate, all find a resting place.

3. *Preoccupation about trifles*: susceptibility irritated by lack of courtesy or consideration of one's seniority of position; pettiness regarding food, clothing, or occupations.

4. *Concern over the opinion of others* and especially the expressed or presumed judgement of superiors. Sometimes a glance or the silence of a superior takes on more importance than her words. A woman knows how to give many different meanings to her silence; her experience and intuition render her very apt to perceive the meaning of the silence of others, especially superiors; her emotional nature will make her very capable of suffering from it, and unless she watches carefully, her prayer will be stifled by it.

To be able to pray, then, the heart must be free, and for this a continual self-denial and struggle against these morose passions are necessary. All that destroys in us peace and joy, the fruits of the Holy Spirit, also destroys the spirit of prayer and the ability to pray.

Mastery over one's feelings is indeed never very rapid nor very complete. It may well be that the heart will boil as a result of injustice, meanness or suffering. The holocaust of a bruised heart must be offered to God together with the feelings in revolt, and this painful and inglorious offering may be the deepest prayer because it is a true participation in the agony of Jesus, and presents to the Father in the night of faith the lowly homage of sorrow and weakness.

But it is quite otherwise with those who with unwholesome delectation nurse their sadness and bitterness in their soul. For them no conversation with God is possible, and God rejects them from his presence.

Distractions born of preoccupation with daily work

If we agree for a moment to divide the day into two parts, a time for prayer and a time for work, which takes precedence over the other, not only in length, but especially in influence? Does love of the Lord, nourished in prayer, gain added vitality as it penetrates the whole of our work? Or is it work that penetrates into the heart of prayer, bringing with it its distractions or rather preoccupations? How many consecrated souls do we not find who are hindered in their prayer by the sheer weight of the work which they had to put aside momentarily for prayer, but towards which they tend with an impatience that makes them count the minutes. How many others transform their prayer into a vestibule of work in which the latter is being prepared and organized!

In this case also it must be said that such distractions are extremely revealing as to the desires of the heart. 'Where your treasure is, there will your heart be also.' Where then is the heart? In God, or in work? Let no one say it is all one, and that the faithful performance of the duties of one's state is a service to God. It may be and often is at the same time a subtle form of self-seeking. Involvement in the duties of one's state often implies an ambiguous motivation. One may at the same time be seeking God and seeking self, loving God and loving self. For this reason action must ceaselessly be purified in the crucible of prayer. So many apostolic or simply material tasks take hold of the entire being and satisfy its aspirations. Duty is a convenient excuse to lull the conscience to sleep. Once again, to whom does the heart belong? If it belongs to God, prayer will not be very much disturbed by distractions arising from work, while the latter will easily be penetrated by prayer. But if the heart is enslaved by work, even of a spiritual or apostolic nature, the face of God will hardly be revealed in prayer.

Many priests and religious will protest on the score of fatigue, the multiplicity of obligations, the increasing demands for competence, etc. All this is true. Nowadays especially, we are in great danger of being engulfed in work. But the most serious temptation to overcome is not that of fatigue, but of a temperament spontaneously inclined to activism, which finds it easier to plunge headfirst into work than to pray, which derives such intoxicating satisfaction from this feverish activity that to God is left only a very secondary place in the depths of the heart.

It is not sufficient to have put on a religious habit, to live in community and say many prayers; it is necessary first of all to give one's heart to God. Without that, what would be the meaning of religious consecration? What would distinguish a nursing sister from a lay nurse? A religious teacher from her lay collaborators?

A battle must be waged daily to disengage the heart's deepest orientation towards God from the pressure of external duties and the anxieties they engender. *To offer our work to God* is not sufficient to solve the problem; the work must be *done with God* and in his presence. A few very simple counsels may help modern apostles to attain this end.

Let them organize their day, listing tasks in order of importance. Foresight, planning—words belonging to the complex of modern efficiency—may well be baptized by modern apostles. The life of many priests and religious gives the impression of perpetual disorder. They are carried away by their occupations like a plank in a stream. How can they worthily offer to the Lord a life which they are unable to grasp firmly? The call of 'urgent tasks' resounds so loud in their ears, that they do not heed the discreet insistence of the truly important and probably less pleasing work which they put off until later.

They must be able to refuse what they cannot do. In religious communities, the responsibility of attending to such matters rests with superiors. The saying 'Ask for nothing, refuse nothing' has been quoted and made to justify either a blind obedience believed for that reason to be supernatural, or else unbridled activity which is taken for generosity. Nothing must be refused to the will of God; this is the true foundation of supernatural obedience. But the true will of God must be sought, as Christ himself 'sought' the will of his Father.

They must let others assist them, and accept the risks of such a delegation of powers. This will be humiliating, sometimes even tormenting. But the responsibility which lies in the interior of the heart must be protected, otherwise there can be no religious consecration. Although I have already spoken at length of the disastrous effects of overwork in the life of religious, I do not hesitate to return to the subject again. With certainty I can state that in many outwardly very worthy and well regulated religious and sacerdotal lives, there has occurred a veritable death by inanition or asphyxiation of the consecrated vocation. The bark remains, but the tree is dead.

Much more is needed than to participate in exercises and to say prayers. We must pray. In order to pray, we must have the time and the strength to do so. Our hearts must be so taken up with God that he will be found in the midst of the most diverse tasks. In order to pray, we must not be so possessed by a thirst for activity that the time of prayer becomes filled with preoccupations concerning work. A form of penance is being sought for our times. It is to be found at the very heart of our life, and its demands proceed from the requirements of God's love. Thus we see once again that unceasing self-denial is necessary if we are to attain or preserve that freedom of heart without which prayer is impossible.

Innocent distractions

When the heart belongs firmly to God there still remains a series of distractions which disturb prayer and are a cause of worry to many religious. These distractions occur only in the psychic area of the soul, the imaginative zone which is never at rest since it produces dreams in one's sleep.

How can distractions be explained? Three comparisons will help us, however approximately, to circumscribe the problem and reduce it gradually to its right and insignificant proportions.

a. We have, at our permanent disposal, a whole host of faculties: intellect, memory, imagination, feelings or emotions, and especially the 'heart' in the sense in which I have already defined it. With these faculties we are like a shepherd among his sheep, which are by nature fairly inconstant and undisciplined. They have been trained to walk in relative order by the education given in the course of meditation. At the moment of entering into the heart of prayer, we gather them round us. Held under obedience by our active presence, all the sheep walk together as far as the threshold of the temple in which the encounter with God takes place. But only the sheep named 'heart' can cross the threshold of the temple, for the heart is the deep willingness which loves, chooses, and pledges itself to the service of God. The other sheep are idle, without occupation and without shepherd at the threshold of prayer. What else can they do but wander about and engender distractions? This does not mean that we must allow them to wander. We must, on the contrary, endeavour to appease and quiet them, but we must also resign ourselves never completely to succeed in doing so.

b. When we start out to visit someone at a definite address, we know very well whence we come and where we are going, and by what route. On the road we meet other persons travelling the same way or in the other direction. We cannot fail to see them for our eyes are open, and this is a good thing because otherwise there might be accidents. All these persons and vehicles which we meet do not turn us away from our goal, nor do they slow down our progress. So it is with innocent distractions; they do not prevent the soul from driving forward to the meeting-place with God. It would be quite otherwise if the heart did not advance energetically to meet God; if it allowed itself to be delayed and captivated by what it saw on the way.

c. A dazzling light blinds and hurts the eyes that are fixed upon it. So it is with the gaze of the soul when it is fixed on God. The meeting with God in prayer places the soul in painful obscurity. The gaze of one who begins to pray is the gaze of a blind man. The true encounter with God takes place in aridity and even in suffering. It is often said in the Bible that one cannot *see God* and live. Must we not recognize that the difficulty we experience in remaining before God in the emptiness of prayer stems from the reactions of our corporeal and sinful being which must die before seeing

God, and suffers from it? Is not aridity in prayer a sort of purgatory preparing the soul for the vision of God?

Thomas Merton writes:

Prayer and love are learned in the hour when prayer has become impossible and your heart has turned to stone.

If you have never had any distractions you don't know how to pray. For the secret of prayer is a hunger for God and for the vision of God, a hunger that lies far deeper than the level of language or affection. And a man whose memory and imagination are persecuting him with a crowd of useless or even evil thoughts and images may sometimes be forced to pray far better, in the depths of his murdered heart, than one whose mind is swimming with clear concepts and brilliant purposes and easy acts of love.

That is why it is useless to get upset when you cannot shake off distractions. In the first place, you must realize that they are often unavoidable in the life of prayer. The necessity of kneeling and suffering submersion under a tidal wave of wild and inane images is one of the standard trials of the contemplative life. If you think you are obliged to stave these things off by using a book and clutching at its sentences the way a drowning man clutches at straws, you have the privilege of doing so, but if you allow your prayer to degenerate into a period of simple spiritual reading you are losing a great deal of fruit. You would profit much more by patiently resisting distractions and learning something of your own helplessness and incapacity. And if your book merely becomes an anaesthetic, far from helping your meditation it has ruined it altogether. . . .

In all these things, it is the will to pray that is the essence of prayer, and the desire to find God and to see him and to love him is the one thing that matters. If you have desired to know him and love him you have already done what was expected of you, and it is much better to desire God without being able to think clearly of him, than to have marvellous thoughts about him without desiring to enter into union with his will.[1]

IV. WHAT ARE THE HELPS TO PRAYER?

In these pages inspired by the frequently disappointing experience of priests and religious endeavouring to practise mental prayer in the midst of a hectic existence, I should like now to suggest a certain number of practical means external to prayer, which would facilitate its practice. Prayer is of capital importance in unifying, through love, a consecrated life; but much of the failure of religious souls in this area where they should normally feel very much at ease, springs from their negligence or inertia in adopting these means.

1. *Commitment and perseverance*

The capital sin against which we should be most on our guard in the spiritual life is neither pride nor sensuality, but sloth. Here indeed lies the major obstacle to prayer. The latter is difficult, arid, and demands hard and selfless effort; to our positive and practical minds it seems to serve no useful purpose. And so any excuse seems good enough to justify shortening or giving up prayer. In fact, at the beginning of prayer, other duties suddenly assume an unsuspected importance which finds in self a stealthy accomplice.[2] But as soon as we have decided not to pray, the interior tension is appeased and we find all the time needed to do useless things.

It is imperative for us to remove the mask from our face

[1] *Seeds of Contemplation* (Norfolk, Conn.: New Directions, 1949), pp. 140-1; 143.

[2] Father Leo Trese cleverly remarks that the half-hour he intends to devote to mental prayer always becomes 'the shortest half-hour of the day' under pressure of circumstances and the complicity of his own laziness. *Vessel of Clay* (New York: Sheed & Ward, 1951), p. 7.

and settle the question once and for all, to avoid having to begin this exhausting struggle again each day. We must be totally committed, and definitely declare the matter closed to discussion.

St Teresa of Avila insisted much on the need for energetic action here, with all the uncompromising definiteness implied in the words. 'Everything is done,' she would say, 'when a soul *decides* to pray.'

But it is not sufficient to decide to begin, we must persevere with the same decision. The great quality needed by those who pray amid dryness and distractions is perseverance. Jesus gave no other directive: '. . . Always to pray and not lose heart' (Luke 18:1). The difficulty he experienced in teaching prayer to his apostles (for example, in the Garden of Olives) did not incite him to reserve it for an elite among religious, of those who would be properly prepared by moderate work and an atmosphere of recollection, and to refuse it to people exhausted with fatigue. Perseverance is the key to prayer, and it depends on one's courage or rather one's love. It is the sign of love, and sometimes the only sign visible to those who walk towards God in dryness and fatigue. A sign of true love, perseverance is also its food.

Here again, in the effort required for such perseverance will be found a form of penance proper to the present day. But if we have the courage to continue, we shall also find therein the true mystical life.

2. *Spiritual reading, the necessary support of prayer*

Spiritual reading is important as a psychological preparation for prayer. Considered from this viewpoint, there are three types of spiritual reading:

a. That which is done in preparation for catechetical instruction. This 'interested' type of reading is of no particular assistance to prayer which must be essentially selfless.

b. Books of solid spiritual doctrine are not foreign to prayer, but their influence is an indirect one. They require sustained intellectual activity and we know that since the prayer of the 'heart' is neither reflection nor meditation, it excludes the action of the intellect.

c. True spiritual reading which efficaciously prepares the way for prayer should be done *daily*, even if only for a few minutes. It must be taken out of a book that is easy to read, and full of the spirit of prayer. What criteria will guide us in choosing such a book? They vary according to the spiritual physiognomy of each soul. But generally these books were written by authors who prayed as they wrote, and who were not always aware that their books would be published. Fundamentally, *the best book is that which inspires us with a desire to pray, and true spiritual reading is prayer begun.*

3. *Preparation for prayer*

The psychological preparation is so important that frequently lack of success in prayer (too easily termed dryness, spiritual trial, or the 'dark night') or even abandoning prayer, comes from an undervaluation of this primordial factor. The contents of our psychological consciousness at the moment when evening is ending and night is about to begin remain actively on the surface of the mind the whole night through. We have all had the experience, at some time in our life, of going to bed obsessed by an insoluble problem, and awakening the next day to find it solved.

At the moment of retiring we must get on the runway and begin moving, as it were, so that the morning's flight in prayer may not be delayed or prevented. Preparation for prayer does not simply consist in an intellectual choice of a subject or a text. The preparation is the beginning of prayer. At the moment of falling asleep, we must be in a state of prayer. Thus sleeplessness itself will not be considered a tragedy, but an opportunity for prayer, provided by the Lord. And if we are so fortunate as to sleep soundly, our first thought on awakening will continue our last thought on falling asleep, with all the enrichment which the subconscious activity of life will have brought. So it is clear that we must not read in bed, and especially not a newspaper or a secular book. Once again, if we seek a form of penance suited to modern times, here is one within our easy grasp.

4. *The examen of conscience*

The examen of conscience is frequently deceiving and badly understood because badly taught. Several errors are often involved in it. Either faults are peeled off in a manner well within the ability of a good pagan with a knowledge of the moral law; or these faults are taken out of their context and made to fit into abstract formulas. Besides, it is often a purely passive and negative process. Finally, it soon becomes superficial since we are easily tempted to be satisfied with an enumeration which appears exhaustive.

The examen of conscience should first of all be a prayer (this should be true of every other spiritual exercise, and indeed of any moment of the day). In order to know ourselves, we must not first place ourselves under a microscope, but in full light, that is, in contemplation before God in love.

Next, we must look for what has really been done for the love of God. If it is true, according to St John of the Cross, that 'in the evening of life we shall be judged on love', what is there, in the evening of this one day, that can be taken up and offered to God as a sign of our love? What will stand his judgement?

Then we must go back to gather the rest in order to offer it in repentance to the mercy of God.

Finally, whatever else may be lacking, we must always end

our examination of conscience with an autopsy of the 'heart', in order to discover if it really tends with all its strength towards God. We easily ask ourselves in an examen of conscience if God is pleased with us, and we have a thousand reasons to conclude that he is not. Why not ask ourselves if we are pleased with him and at his service, and if our heart possesses that peace and that joy which, says Saint Paul, are the fruits of the Holy Spirit?

Once again, I do not intend to write a complete treatise on prayer. Excellent books have been written and I could only repeat what they have said. Besides, nothing is better than direct contact with truly spiritual persons who have known God and have told what they learned, stammeringly it may be, but with wondrous and disturbing effects. Julien Green wrote of an ecclesiastic who was compiling a treatise on mysticism:

> He has the honesty of admitting at the outset that he has never experienced any of the things he is about to describe. In a word, he intends to write a book about China, where he has never set foot, with the use of books that have been written about this country. I had rather read Saint Teresa, who at least has made the journey.[1]

Each must try to find her own way to God, following in the steps of those who have found him and or whom the Church approves.

The aim of this chapter has been simply to give some practical advice on prayer to priests and religious carrying heavy material burdens, for prayer should be for them the primary principle of unification. With regard to ways of prayer and food for prayer, however, it will be for each

[1] Julien Green, *Journal*, 'Le Bel Aujourd'hui' (Paris: Plon), p. 282.

religious family to draw upon its own spiritual resources. It belongs especially to the Holy Spirit, the teacher of prayer, to furnish light and strength; but we must humbly co-operate with him by making use of human means, with the courage of a steadfast will.

7

A School of Fraternal Charity According to the Gospel

Bear one another's burdens, and so fulfill the law of Christ.

Gal. 6:2

Through love be servants of one another.

Gal. 5:13

The more brotherly love increases, the greater is love for God; and the more divine love increases, the greater also is love for the neighbour, since both have the same source and the same cause.

Saint John of the Cross, *Ascent of Mount Carmel*, Bk. III, Ch. 23.

I SHOULD LIKE to insist in this chapter on the major importance of fraternal charity as an ascetical and mystical element of religious life, as a source of affective and psychological equilibrium, as a bond of peace in communities, and as a condition of the witness which consecrated persons are called to give in the dechristianized world in which they exercise their apostolate.

It does not come about easily in certain religious families. Community life can be a source of acute suffering especially for a woman, whose keener emotions combined with her capacity to suffer renders her painfully aware of a word, a glance, or an attitude, or of the silence or an oversight of others. In religious life, dependence on superiors is very close and contacts with others are frequent. Because of the proximity in which sisters live, small hurts never have time to heal; on the contrary, the necessary practice of communal living constantly irritates old wounds. All this is human, humiliating, and often very painful. Unless she is careful, a sister may allow the whole field of her psychological consciousness to be invaded by these small problems which are often imaginary, except for her who suffers them.

The situation is more serious than is generally believed, for herein probably resides one of the causes of decline in religious vocations. Girls are quick to notice irritability among members of a religious community, and they shudder at the thought of spending their lifetime in such an atmosphere. With a Christian conscience refined by feminine intuition and sensibility, they are aware of the fact that fraternal charity is the sign of genuine consecration to the Lord, and conversely, that love of God without love of others is purely pharisaical pretence—and they draw their own conclusions.

The formation of novices in fraternal charity is often insufficient, and the instruction given later by superiors easily assumes a moralizing tone. Priests usually speak emphatically on this subject in retreats and conferences, but there is a lack of co-ordination and organization in all these efforts, as well as a want of clear insight into the successive stages through which the goal is reached. There is lacking especially *the conviction that fraternal charity must be taught during the whole of religious life*, by the patient efforts of those who have authority in the name of the Church.

Fraternal charity is often considered merely as one virtue among others, even when it is given first place and bound up with love of God. It is much more than a virtue; it is the whole of the spiritual life. It is, indeed, *a form of asceticism* in the sense that it cannot grow unless the heart is completely stripped of its instinctive selfishness. This entails a veritable dying through humility, which is a condition for the growth of brotherly love. For although the latter is first in dignity (along with love of God, the 'first commandment'), it is not first in the logical or psychological order.

Fraternal charity is also *mystical* in the sense that it can flourish only in faith. It causes one to love the Lord in persons, or better still, to love persons with the heart of the Lord. It should become a true path to contemplation, perhaps the most rapid, at any rate the least subject to illusions. Those who are not alert to the need of unceasing progress in brotherly love and who do not constantly learn new things about it should rightly be concerned, for they are asleep.

It is hardly necessary to point out that sins against charity, even grave ones, are more easily committed than others against which conscience is alerted rather by scruples than by spiritual sensitivity. Jesus' prophecy of the last judgement shows sins of omission in this matter as punishable by eternal fire (Matt. 25).

Christians are generally not aware of the capital importance of brotherly love; this is evident in the manner in which they examine their conscience and confess their sins. The majority of priests and religious are hardly more perceptive in this matter. We may plead at the last judgement that we did not know. The word of the Lord will reply: You had 'Moses and the prophets' (Luke 16 : 29). You had the Gospels. But how many read the Gospels to find a way of life therein? How many follow literally its astonishing doctrine? As an echo of the teaching of Jesus, St John writes:

He who says he is in the light and hates his brother is

in the darkness still. He who loves his brother abides in
the light, and in him there is no cause for stumbling. But
he who hates his brother is in the darkness and walks in the
darkness, and does not know where he is going, because
the darkness has blinded his eyes (I John 2:9-11).

There is a long road to cover in learning to love others.
The starting point (loving one's neighbour as *oneself*) seems
to be within the ability of man, but the point of arrival is
inaccessible to human strength (loving one's neighbour *as
Jesus loves him*). It is by this we know that brotherly love is
the work of grace, and depends on the living intensity of
divine love in us.

But it also depends on humble human effort, particularly
of superiors and those in charge of sister formation. In this
endeavour they are not left to their own devices. They have
a textbook—the Gospels; and we shall briefly study the
various stages to be covered in teaching brotherly love as
embracing all of the religious life.

For the Lord has spoken; he trained the apostles, and in
his teaching may be discerned the stages of true pedagogy.
His was not a systematized method; but with the passing of
time Christ demanded more of them in this sense, that the
motives of their love were more and more elevated.

I. THE STARTING POINT OF FRATERNAL CHARITY

'. . . as yourself.'

Mark 12:31

Jesus begins the instruction of his disciples at the point
where the Old Testament leaves off, directing them to love
others as they love themselves. The scene as described by
the evangelists is well known.

And one of the scribes came up and heard them disputing with one another, and seeing that he answered them well, asked him, 'Which commandment is the first of all?' Jesus answered, 'The first is, 'Hear, O Israel: The Lord our God, the Lord is one; and you shall love the Lord your God with all your heart, and with all your soul, and with all your mind, and with all your strength." The second is this, 'You shall love your neighbour as yourself.' There is no other commandment greater than these.' And the scribe said to him, 'You are right, Teacher; you have truly said that he is one, and there is no other but he; and to love him with all the heart, and with all the understanding, and with all the strength, and to love one's neighbour as oneself, is much more than all whole burnt offerings and sacrifices (Mark 12:28-33).

We notice here that Jesus does not address himself directly to his disciples, but to a scribe. However, each of his gestures, words, and miracles, is intended for the apostles who surround him as well as for his immediate interlocutor. It is their formation with which he is primarily concerned, and which is described in the Gospels.

So intimately is love of God above all things linked with love of neighbour, that it was on being asked about the first commandment alone that Jesus said, 'Love your neighbour as yourself.' There can be no fraternal charity unless it is inspired by the love of God; neither will there ever be any authentic love of God unless it is expressed in love of others.

Although it is only a beginning, love of others 'as oneself' must not be minimized. A wholesome love of self is necessary in order maturely and fully to love others. Christ further explains this first step when he says, 'Whatever you wish that men would do to you, do so to them' (Matt. 7:12).

II. FIRST OBSTACLE: PRIDE, AND THE STAGE OF HUMILITY

'I have given you an example . . .'

John 13:15

Taking as their guide (and rightly so) the words of Jesus, 'Truly, I say to you, as you did it to one of the least of these my brethren, you did it to me' (Matt. 25:40), Christians and especially religious often try to discover the mysterious presence of Jesus in others, and are surprised at their failure to make progress in this way. They are not precisely going too fast, but they do not take into consideration certain psychological and spiritual realities; they are neglecting the self-discipline of humility.

Humility before God

It is remarkable how frequently in the Gospel Jesus contrasts two types of persons: the pharisee and the publican, the elder son and the prodigal, Simon and the sinful woman.

In the parable of the pharisee and the publican, for example, the one is full of all virtues and sure of his worth, with reason it would seem; but *he stands before God*, treating with him as with an equal, pointing a finger of scorn at the publican. The latter on the contrary, 'would not even lift up his eyes to heaven, but beat his breast, saying, "God, be merciful to me a sinner!"' (Luke 18:13). His heart was so full of the consciousness of his misery that it was impossible for him to condemn the other. What a profound lesson there is in this! It is impossible for a man ever to achieve an indulgent fraternal charity if he has not first humbled himself profoundly before God in the consciousness of his own misery.

Very often Christians (and religious) pass judgement upon

others, applying no other criterion than the secret conviction of their own virtue and good standing before God. Sometimes their conscience will trouble them, so they resolve to correct this tendency to condemn others; but they soon fall back into the same fault. They will never learn to judge indulgently until they rid themselves of their pharisaic mentality. If they once bow down in the dust before God, their heart will be renewed and they will be capable of loving. Once again it is evident that every stage of brotherly love becomes an encounter with the Lord, for indulgence towards others is the only authentic attitude of a sinner conscious of his own wretchedness before God.

This must be taught in the noviceship and at every level of religious formation. Fraternal charity is, I repeat, more than a virtue; it is all of the Christian life. It is beyond our limited efforts and the reassurance inspired by our good resolutions. Genuine fraternal charity implies *knowledge of God*, an acute sense of his greatness, his power, and his glory, and a deep sense of our personal wretchedness (cf. Is. 6:5 and Job 42:5-6). He who is convinced of his sinfulness has not the courage to condemn others.

Humility before others

Formation in fraternal charity implies that religious begin to learn humility towards others in the noviceship. Here again we are taught by the words and actions of Jesus. At the very moment he was to promulgate solemnly the charter of fraternal charity, before praying solemnly for unity among his apostles so that they might be his witnesses, before founding his Church and entrusting its government to human hands, Jesus knelt before his disciples and washed their feet, 'I have given you an example, that you also should do as I have done to you' (John 13:15).

It is indeed true that pride is the principal obstacle to brotherly love, and we never finish learning humility. It will perhaps be observed that the whole of religious life is a school of humility, which is learned by means of humiliations. This remains to be proved. Why make a goal of humility? It is but a means to the end, which is love. Like all the virtues, humility is a reflection of Christ; it reproduces the humility of Christ, meek and humble of heart. And in his disciples humility is the means and the key to brotherly love: 'I have given you an example.'

To be capable of growing in fraternal love, the heart must be rid of the pride that encumbers it; and to die to pride, one must live in spirit at the feet of others. Humility is also the means of creating unity in a community;[1] it is the condition of an unselfish apostolate; finally, it is the only way of exercising authority in the Church.

III. THE OBSTACLE OF EXCLUSIVENESS AND THE RADICALISM OF CHARITY

'The least of these my brethren.'

Matt. 25:40

What often kills fraternal charity is the choice of some to the exclusion of others, the elimination of one or of a category of persons from the circle of love. Nothing is more contrary to the teaching of Jesus. In summarizing his teaching we shall endeavour to recapture its original emphasis.

---

[1] In exhorting the Philippians to unity, St Paul urges them: 'Do nothing from selfishness or conceit, but in humility count others better than yourselves'; and he invites them to have among themselves the same mind as Jesus Christ, who 'emptied himself, taking the form of a servant. . . and became obedient unto death, even death on a cross' (Phil. 2:3-8).

Jesus admits of no exception; charity *must be universal*, for all are children of the Father (cf. Matt. 5:43-55). Jesus invites us to the perfection of a love that forgets no one when he says, 'You, therefore, must be perfect as your heavenly Father is perfect'.

We see once again that at every stage of our education in brotherly love, we encounter the face of God; for how can brothers learn to love one another without an increasing awareness of being children of a common Father? Since the Father loves all his children, none must exclude a brother from his heart. So that his disciples may be under no delusions, Jesus goes into detail.

They must love *the most abandoned*, the hungry, the thirsty, strangers, the naked, the sick, even evildoers in prison (Matt. 25:35-6). In our society all these misfortunes bear modern names with the consequent risk of hiding their evangelical reality, but if we open our eyes we shall recognize them. Jesus embraces them all in the wondrous expression, 'the least of these my brethren'. The tenderness of the Lord and the dignity of these 'least' are a permanent invitation to seek out all of them in the obscurity in which they live hidden from the sight of the self-righteous whose conscience is at peace.

The most ill-disposed must also be loved. Community life reveals them readily and provides alert educators with the opportunity of guiding their religious into strong and wholesome ways of spiritual asceticism. It is easy to love our friends —even pagans can do that. We must love our enemies. Jesus details various categories of enemies: those who hate, curse, abuse and strike others; appropriators (Luke 6:27-30) and troublemakers (Matt. 5:40).

Commentaries on Luke 6:27-35 or Matthew 5:38-48 will, in the concrete circumstances of community life, assume a singular value. Likewise that on Matthew 5:22-4; for the words of Jesus are terribly exacting and should be pondered deeply. 'So if you are offering your gift at the altar, and there remember that your brother has something against you . . .' It is the brother who is at fault that needs love.

Does it ever happen in religious communities that two sisters estranged by resentment refrain from receiving Communion? If, from the beginning of their religious life, they are imbued with the sacred character of brotherly love and its intimate connection with the sacrifice of the Mass, daily Communion will nourish charity; and when a difficulty arises, it will become an urgent motive for reconciliation. Why allow the Gospel message to be so watered down for many consecrated souls, that they lose their keenness to perceive that a heart where fraternal love does not reign, far from being a shelter, becomes a prison for the Body of Christ.

IV. REALISTIC BROTHERLY LOVE AFTER THE MANNER OF JESUS

'Love one another; even as I have loved you.'

John 13:34

It is well to ponder these words at length, for we know them so well that we no longer understand them in our heart. It was not until the very end of her life that St Teresa of Lisieux, holy as she was, understood them fully. Three months before her death, June 1897, she wrote:

Among the countless graces I have received this year, perhaps the greatest has been that of being able to grasp in all its fulness the meaning of charity. I had never before fathomed Our Lord's words: The second commandment is LIKE the first: 'You shall love your neighbour as yourself' (Matt. 22:39). I had striven above all to love God, and in loving Him I discovered the secret of those other words: 'Not every one who says to me, "Lord, Lord," shall enter the kingdom of heaven, but he who does the will of my Father who is in heaven' (Matt. 7:21). Jesus made me understand what this will was by the words He used at the Last Supper when He gave His 'new commandment' and told His apostles to love one another as He had loved them. I began to consider just how Jesus had loved His disciples. I saw it was not for their natural qualities for I recognized they were ignorant men and often preoccupied with earthly affairs. Yet He calls them His friends and His brethren. He wants to see them near Him in the kingdom of His Father and to open this kingdom to them He wills to die on the Cross, saying: 'Greater love has no man than this, that a man lay down his life for his friends' (John 15:13). As I meditated on these words of Jesus, I saw how imperfect was my love for the other nuns and I knew that I did not love them as Jesus loves them. But now I realize that true charity consists in putting up with all one's neighbours faults, never being surprised by his weakness, and being inspired by the least of his virtues. Above all, I learnt that charity is not something that stays shut up in one's heart, for men do not light a candle and 'put it under a bushel, but on a stand, and it gives light to all in the house' (Matt. 5:15). This candle represents that charity which must illumine and cheer not only those dearest to me but 'all in the house'.[1]

These words of Jesus, 'as I have loved you', should be a light to us; but they can also be a flame consuming the instinctive selfishness which prevents the growth of love. How has Jesus loved us?

a. *He loved us first* (I John 4:19). He loved the apostles

[1] *Manuscrits autobiographiques*, pp. 263-5. *The Autobiography of St Teresa of Lisieux*, Tr. John Beevers (New York: Doubleday, 1957), pp. 121-2.

just as they were, not in spite of their defects, but even *because of them*. He loved them because he is good, and love made them good as it can make us good.

The realism of Christ's love must be understood and taken seriously. He loved his apostles such as they were, and he loves us such as we are. 'God shows his love for us in that while we were yet sinners Christ died for us,' says Saint Paul (Rom. 5:8).

It is often before this obstacle that brotherly love fails in religious communities. We admit theoretically that others may have defects (just as we have ourselves) but it is quite otherwise when we have daily practical experience of these defects. We are incapable of loving those who are unpleasant, unloving, irritating. Should conscience reproach us, we try to be pleasant, we 'act as if' we loved them, and dispense ourselves from seeing them as they are and accepting their poverty. Yet Jesus loved his apostles and loves us with realism. He loved his executioners with the same realism: 'Father, forgive them; for they know not what they do' (Luke 23:34).

This realistic love of Jesus is the measure of the brotherly love which he commands: 'A new commandment I give to you, that you love one another; even as I have loved you, that you also love one another' (John 13:34).

Christ's love is always the same, since it is in our present condition that he saves us; this truth should be a constant subject of contemplation for religious. If not, what they term 'fraternal charity' runs the risk of being nothing but hypocrisy.

We must love others first, not because they are good, but because the goodness of the Father is in us, because 'the love of Christ impells us'. We must love our enemies (those whom we believe to be such), not because they are our enemies, but in order that they may no longer be so, just as merciful love comes to us sinners, in order to cure us of sin.

b. *Jesus loved us 'to the end'* (John 13:1), that is, to the very limit of love. 'Greater love has no man than this, that a man lay down his life for his friends' (John 15:13). According to St Paul, Jesus' sacrifice of his life for the Church is the model for true conjugal love: 'Husbands, love your wives, as Christ loved the church and gave himself up for her' (Eph. 5:25). In the heart of a Christian (how much more of a religious) love is genuine only if it is willing to go thus far—to the daily giving of its life.

Let us be practical. How can we, in community, feel and exercise a love such as this? Just as the love of Jesus involves the gift of his person, so our love for others is the offering of our person. It is first not an act, but a state; not an effort of the will, but a daily offering of ourselves. Acts of charity are nothing unless they are inspired by a permanent disposition to love. Nor does love spring from a sense of duty or a human will to do good; it is the necessary, spontaneous, and selfless fruit of an inner life. When a mother watches through the night at the bedside of a sick child, she does not feel that she is doing anything extraordinary, for she is the mother. So should it be for supernatural fraternal charity.

A religious community is made up of a superior and a group of sisters. The relationships existing between them in virtue of their respective functions are non-essential. What is essential is the fact that they are all daughters of a common Father: this is a relationship of communion. Functional relationships are always transitory and depend on eventual appointments; whereas relationships of communion are definitive, depending on the same baptism, renewed at the same religious profession. The relationship of a superior with her sisters lasts only as long as her term of office. But as to the relationships of communion according to which she is the sister of all in Christ, these are essential and must permeate with selflessness everything that she does in her community life. Loving must be as normal to her as living and breathing, day after day until her death.

So should it be for every religious; and training in this regard should be tirelessly pursued through the noviceship and during all of the religious life. In this area will be found concrete evidence of the link that exists between affective maturity and true fraternal charity. We shall have occasion to speak of the opportunities afforded by daily sufferings and difficulties for the formation of sisters to a spirit of faith; but we may here remark that some spiritual lives are broken and die beneath the trials of common life. True, these sisters entered religion to love the Lord and to love others; but they also desired, more or less consciously, to be loved and understood. As a result in religious life there sometimes develop affective deviations proper to adolescents: inordinate attachment to a superior, who becomes the substitute for a sister's mother, whose 'little girl' she remains indefinitely; a bond of exclusive friendship with a sister who serves as confidante and recipient of personal problems which always fill her mind; antipathy towards those who have hurt her or who simply ignore her.

Candidates to the religious life must be taught during the novitiate and all their lives that love seeks to give itself without awaiting the other's initiative. They must learn that love is a gift to others, a gift or a state such that it receives (and that abundantly) only in the measure in which it is spontaneous. This requires a continual education and it calls for the support of a rigorous self-denial. The perfection of love is attained by a consecrated soul only when, in the midst of deep personal grief, she can go out of herself to others, all others, especially if among them should be found the agents of her suffering. Such love cannot be understood nor attained without a special grace granted to urgent prayer. We realize once again that fraternal charity involves all of the spiritual life and brings about unity in the mystical life. It is an authentic and safe way of contemplation. Saint Teresa of Lisieux writes at the conclusion of the text quoted above:

> O Jesus, I know you command nothing that is impossible. You know how weak and imperfect I am, and you know only too well that I could never love the other nuns as you love them if you yourself did not love them *within me*. . . .
> When I act and think with charity, I feel it is Jesus who works within me. The closer I am united with him, the more I love all the other dwellers in Carmel.[1]

To become able to understand and practise such love, it is necessary to pray much and live in contemplation. Within the mystery of intimate union with the Father through Jesus Christ in the Holy Spirit, a religious discovers that there is only one love: that which unites her with God and overflows continually upon others.

Thus we understand that fraternal charity must be affectionate and tender, and not be deprived of the warmth of sentiment. Of course, there is some risk of affective deviations; but can there be true Christian education without risk? It is possible to show affection without giving demonstrations of it. Besides, she who loves everyone with her whole heart is much more likely to be well balanced than one who is constantly on her guard and restraining herself. Did not our Lord love the apostles in this open, relaxed and affectionate manner? Human beings need affection more

[1] *Ibid.*, p. 123.

than they need bread, and even in religious communities, there are those whose hearts are dying of starvation. This hunger for affection, not inspired by emotion but by the love of the Lord burning in the heart, carries with it its own continual purification, for it is not often repaid.

V. DISCOVERING CHRIST IN OTHERS

'As you did it to one of the least of these, my brethren, you did it to me.'

Matt. 25:40

It is now possible for us to understand this saying of Jesus in the light of God. Every form of fraternal charity in the Church for the past twenty centuries has been inspired by this prophecy of the last judgement.

The word of Jesus is a divine word, effecting what it signifies. Jesus did not say, 'It is as if you did it to me', but 'You did it *to me.*' Fraternal charity has a quasi-sacramental force. By it Christ becomes present. Others are not a reflection of Christ, *they are Christ* for one who lives by faith.

Once again we discover the marvellous unity of the love of God and of our neighbour. He who lives by faith will easily learn to discern the face of Christ in his brother, and it will be impossible for him to exclude anyone from his love, or even to hold him at a distance. 'If any one says, "I love God", and hates his brother, he is a liar; for he who does not love his brother whom he has seen, cannot love God whom he has not seen' (I John 4:20).

We love God only as much as we love the person we love least; and if we exclude anyone from our love, we have excluded Christ. This principle is solidly founded on the word of God, and it is better to understand and apply it now at any price, than to be compelled to understand it when we

appear before God. 'This commandment we have from him,
that he who loves God should love his brother also' (I John
4:21).

VI. ABIDING IN LOVE

'As the Father has loved me, so have I loved you; abide in my
love. . . . This I command you, to love one another.'

John 15:9,17

We have seen that brotherly love is not merely a virtue,
even of the first rank. It is the very life of God, for 'God is
love' (I John 4:8,16), and 'all love comes from God' (I John
4:7).

From the heart of the Father flows a stream of living
water, the river of love, which fills the heart of the Son:
'The Father has loved me.' From the heart of Christ, this
river flows into the heart of every Christian: 'So have I loved
you.' The Christian is invited to let it permeate his soul
permanently: 'Abide in my love.' Finally, from our heart
the river of love must flow towards all those confided to us
by God: 'Love one another.'

Fraternal charity is then not only a gift but a *sharing*, an
exchange. He who is love, whose very nature it is to love,
untiringly asks for our love. This is the meaning of devotion
to the Sacred Heart. In like manner we need others in order
that God's plan may be realized in us. There is never any
superiority nor condescension in brotherly love; no intention of 'doing good'. For him who really loves God, there
is rather gratitude to those who accept to be loved by
him.

VII. THE EUCHARIST, DAILY FOOD OF BROTHERLY LOVE

'The bread which we break, is it not a participation in the body of Christ? Because there is one bread, we who are many are one body, for we all partake of the one bread.'

I Cor. 10: 16-17

In the course of the religious life, education in fraternal charity is daily nourished by participation in the holy Sacrifice of the Mass and in Communion.

Communion absolutely demands the complete reconciliation of divided hearts. 'If you are offering your gift at the altar and there remember that your brother has something against you . . .' (Matt. 5:23-4). The solemn moment in which one prepares for the encounter with God in the Eucharist is no time for compromise. It is a delusion to say that we love God above all things when we refuse to love the brethren. God does not make difficulties; we can easily have the illusion that we love him. But with our neighbour it is not so easy, in this sense that he is always before us with his defects. It is he whom we must love realistically in order to have the right to say to God, 'I love you'. We must be at one with our neighbour in order to be at one in communion with God.

Of set purpose Jesus firmly promulgated the commandment of fraternal charity with all its implications and exigencies, at the very moment when he was instituting the sacrament of the Eucharist. The baptized Christian is invited to sit at three tables in succession, and partake each time of suitable food.

There is first the table of our human brothers, the table of sinners, at which Jesus sat so often[1] and where charity

[1] Cana (John 2); the vocation of Matthew (Matt. 9:9); Zaccheus (Luke 19:5); Simon the Pharisee (Luke 7:36); the paschal meal (Luke 22:14); Emmaus (Luke 24:30).

134

founded on humility should find a simple expression in community life (Luke 14:7; I Cor. 11). At this table we eat bread, the daily bread, which a child confidently asks of his father (Luke 11:11), which a child of God asks of his heavenly Father, and which Jesus shared with his own.

Then there is the table of the paschal meal prepared in advance, before which Jesus washed the feet of his disciples and where he promulgated the commandments of love. At this table he took bread, transformed it into his Body, and gave it to his disciples to eat. The paschal meal is served again at this table. The Mass is not primarily the renewal of Calvary's sacrifice; it is first of all the re-enactment of Maundy Thursday, the place where all who are present hear the ceaseless promulgation of the precept of the Lord. The altar is the banquet table to which Jesus invites us; the table covered with a cloth on which are placed objects needed for a meal. 'The bread which I shall give for the life of the world is my flesh' (John 6:51). 'The bread which we break, is it not a participation in the body of Christ? Because there is one bread, we who are many are one body, for we all partake of the one bread' (I Cor. 10:16-7).

Finally, there is the table of heaven: 'Blessed is he who shall eat bread in the kingdom of God!' (Luke 14:15). 'Blessed are those who are invited to the marriage supper of the Lamb' (Apoc. 19:9). The simple bread of the first table, having become the flesh of the Lord at the second, is here eternal life. 'He who eats my flesh . . . has eternal life, and I will raise him up at the last day' (John 6:54).

Each table prefigures the next, each bread given as food is a sign of that which is to come, and above all, the eucharistic table is the promise and the pledge of that which is prepared for us.

A Christian community is created and cemented together

through the members' participation in the Eucharist. What then shall we say of a community of sisters in which mutual love is nourished daily by Mass and Communion? This charity is a daily growth promoted by the Body of Christ. Thus it is not a simple duty whose execution depends upon the efforts and the good will of each one. The Lord himself takes charge of it in the hearts of those who accept the exacting significance of their eucharistic life, and its daily renewed supply of grace.

Fraternal charity is, as we have said, the authentic sign of normal growth in a religious vocation. It is the serious duty of all those who have received authority in the name of the Church to see that this growth does in fact take place.

It is, besides, the necessary condition for all effective apostolate. 'By this all men will know that you are my disciples, if you have love for one another' (John 13:35). The witness that draws men to Christ is not that of charity in action, but of the charity that unites the apostles. For this unity Jesus earnestly prayed to His Father: 'That they may all be one . . . so that the world may believe that thou hast sent me . . .' 'That they may become perfectly one, so that the world may know that thou hast sent me . . .' (John 17:21,23).

Love is so important that there can be neither religious life nor apostolate without its continual growth unto fruition.

In every Congregation the sisters should pray unceasingly for an increase of fraternal charity. It would be a great grace if one or several religious from each community would make this the centre of their life of prayer. Without being aware of it perhaps, they would exert an influence on their sisters and become a leaven of love which, after penetrating the dough of their religious family, would bring to the world in which they live the authentic leaven of Christ.

In this world there are two parts: love on one side, and everything else on the other. One can lose all the rest and easily do without it, but one cannot lose love without dying. He who has begun to understand this already abides in the light and has begun his eternity.

8

Understanding the Cross

'Oh foolish men . . . Was it not necessary that the Christ should suffer these things and enter into his glory?'

Luke 24:25-6

A PRIEST who had devoted the greater part of his sacerdotal life to the service of religious communities said during his last illness, 'I believe more and more in the grandeur of religious consecration; but my experience has convinced me that only a limited number of priests and religious make a success of their life. The cause of the failure of the others is to be found in a cross they do not accept, and the one which most frequently proves a stumbling block to them is a change of work, or a disappointment in the apostolate.' He lays stress on one of the causes of suffering in the life of persons consecrated to God, overlooking perhaps the daily suffering of the heart occasioned by living in community.

There is an expression that occurs frequently in the religious vocabulary; it is 'spirit of faith'. A person has a spirit of faith if she can withstand conflicts with circumstances and people, and emerge in hope. She has no spirit of faith if she allows herself to be overwhelmed by sadness and discouragement.

Faith means not only adhesion to a body of revealed truths, nor even simple adhesion to the person of Jesus; it means daily and hourly adhesion to Christ crucified. Saint

138

Paul vigorously defined such faith: 'Far be it from me to glory except in the cross of our Lord Jesus Christ, by which the world has been crucified to me, and I to the world' (Gal. 6:14).

To have a spirit of faith is to recognize the cross of Jesus ever more clearly in all the events of life, until the day on which he invites us to be crucified and die with him, and we consent with mingled agony of heart and response to love.

To have a spirit of faith is to gamble away our life at God's word after the example of the Lord, fully aware that we must necessarily be crucified with him. It is to recognize the cross while it is yet at a distance, under the disconcerting and very humble disguises that it often assumes, to accept being sometimes submerged in grief and anguish, yet hold fast in utter faithfulness to Christ crucified.

'Understanding' the cross is the supernatural faculty of recognizing it and accepting its inevitability, while holding fast to hope in the resurrection: 'Was it not necessary that the Christ should suffer these things and enter into his glory?'

I. THIS WAY MUST BE MADE CLEAR FROM THE BEGINNING OF THE NOVITIATE

1. From the very beginning of their religious life, aspirants must start learning that *a consecrated life is a true participation in the death and resurrection of Jesus*, and that it has no meaning unless this destiny is deliberately accepted. This teaching should not be modified or veiled in the name of human prudence. Why does a girl enter the novitiate? To save souls through teaching and nursing? No doubt. To consecrate herself to God? Yes. But all this is incomplete and

risks deceiving a candidate as it reassures her. She enters in order to allow Christ, truly dead and truly risen, to possess her entirely, 'as a new humanity in which he renews all his mysteries' (Sister Elizabeth of the Trinity). And if certain ungenerous souls are unable to accept this doctrine and choose to fulfil their destiny elsewhere, perhaps this is better for the Church and to the advantage of the individual (though this is hard to see, for the vocation of every Christian is to suffer).

The quality of a religious formation depends on the emphasis given to this teaching. How frequently Jesus said that the disciple is not greater than his master. He did not mince words, and he said it often enough to be understood by the dullest of heart. There was hardly a moment of passing success in his life that was not followed by a prediction of his sufferings and death. The first miracle at Cana in which he 'manifested his glory' (John 2:11), was followed by a veiled prophecy of his Passion (John 2:19); the miracle of the multiplication of the loaves (John 6), by further references to the cross (John 6:51,62); Peter's profession of faith and the proclamation of his primacy (Matt. 16:16-20), by the announcement of his death and resurrection (Matt. 16:21). He did the same after the Transfiguration (Luke 9:28-36), and after the resurrection of Lazarus (John 11; 12:7-8). He wanted to prevent his disciples' limiting their ambitions, even spiritual ones, to merely human accomplishments and hopes of too natural success and efficacy.

Yet in spite of all his efforts, he did not succeed in opening their understanding to the mystery of the cross. The apostles had an excuse; they knew Moses and the prophets (Luke 24:25-7), and in particular Isaiah's description of the suffering Servant (Is. 53), and the complaint of this Servant expressed in Psalm 22 ('My God, my God, why hast thou forsaken me?'); but they were the first to encounter the shock of the mysterious and paradoxical death of the Messiah, this triumph out of failure, a resurrection following upon death and swallowing it up (I Cor. 15:54). It is understandable that they were bewildered by the event.

Consecrated souls should from the very start have a firm notion of what awaits them. It may not be a clear notion, for this can be acquired only through the experience of a lifetime; but to be a bride of Christ means to share something of his own awareness of the way he was to go.

Jesus lived all his earthly life in expectation of his passion, and it must be admitted, in fear of this hour. Many of his words and actions can be understood only in this perspective. Thus the incident in Jerusalem when he was twelve has as its purpose, not only to single out the holy city as a place of conflict and contradiction, but also to prepare his mother for the three days that were to separate his death from his resurrection. In like manner the words to his mother at Cana, 'My hour has not yet come' (John 2:4), referred to the hour of his passion and glorification. We have here a key to help us understand the words of Jesus. He was always thinking of his cruel death, sometimes with anguish (John 12:23-6), always very seriously; and many of his words reflect this thought and this anguish.

The blessed Virgin Mary had the austere privilege of being the only one to share in her Son's foreknowledge of his death. She knew from the beginning that Jesus would be a sign of contradiction and that a sword would pierce her own soul (Luke 2:34-5). Her life of consecration was henceforth to be filled with this prevision of sorrow. Yet she was able to be silent and 'kept all these things in her heart' (Luke 2:51). At Cana she understood the veiled proposal made by her Son, 'My hour has not yet come' (John 2:4); that he gave no further explanation shows that he knew she understood his meaning. For Mary, the loss of Jesus in the temple and the episode of Cana were milestones along a way very familiar to her from the beginning. By the will of God she had been warned as clearly as possible, and her strong and silent presence at the foot of the cross was the fruit of such an education given by the Holy Spirit.

It is important that young sisters should not be deceived on this point by an over-prudent formation. I repeat, the seriousness of a formation programme and the development of individual vocations depend upon the emphasis given to the lessons of the cross. If a dedicated religious surrenders herself in this spirit, the Lord will accept her offering and will lead her by the way of Calvary to participation in his mystery.

It will also be necessary to state with equal force that if Christ has died, he has also risen. Equal emphasis must be given to both phases of the one mystery. Just as formerly there was danger of forgetting the second, the tendency to-day seems to be to pay little attention to the first. We must not forget the necessity of his death: 'Was it not *necessary* that the Christ should suffer . . .' Besides, the resurrection is already at work in the sign of death. 'Death is swallowed up in victory' (I Cor. 15:54).

2. The mystery of Christ which the religious is called to relive will include the work of her *apostolate*. For the apostolate means far more than the communication of a spiritual message; more than human adaptation, professional competence, and commitment in the modern world. This apostolate is a 'redemption' which takes place on the plane of the supernatural. It is important to view the entire plan of God, for the conversion of souls is affected simultaneously on every plane: on the material plane sometimes by the pre-

paration of the ground; on the plane of hearts and intellects by means of ever renewed professional competence (cf. Rom. 10 : 14); on the mysterious plane in which grace acts, where souls are converted ('redeemed') through the suffering of the apostle (cf. Heb. 9 : 22).

Christ continues to save the world through consecrated religious. Today as at every stage in the long history of the Church, the blood of Jesus continues to flow through his members who are called to martyrdom. But his agony is also continued in the person of his apostles—Christians, religious, or priests—who are willing to take their incorporation in the Lord seriously, and to follow it through to the end.

3. Religious must learn from the beginning that *all of life, in all its aspects*, will be marked by the cross. All the personal accomplishments which are demanded of postulants or acquired later through the Congregation, will appear to be taken from them, or rather will have to pass through the cross.

They have good health and it is their duty to take care of it; but fatigue and unforeseen illnesses will eventually affect it until finally old age, which always comes sooner than we think, leads to a death more rapid than we expected.

Their family, which they have indeed given up, but which they still visit from time to time, will gradually be taken from them either by death or by changes occasioned by the passage of time, and they will be left alone.

They have friendships—holy ties will be formed within the Congregation; there again the cross will come, sometimes in ways bitterly painful to human nature. But if they know and expect it, they will recognize it when it comes and be able to bear it in silence, until it becomes transformed by their willingness to sacrifice.

Their spiritual life will grow normally, but their love of the Lord will have to pass through a series of deserts and sometimes very painful spiritual trials. Again, if they expect this, they will not be surprised at certain derelictions, certain 'nights'. When they feel themselves abandoned even by God they will remember the cry of Jesus on the cross, provided this 'lamp shining in a dark place' (II Peter 1 : 19) has been lighted early in their religious life.

They have talents which will be developed within the Congregation; but even these must be purified, for God does not wish anyone to attribute to himself what he has lent for the service of others.

Their apostolate itself will be marked by the cross, sometimes in the most humiliating and disconcerting ways. It will come not only from fatigue and the weight of responsibility, but from the very persons for whom they are labouring. What is even more cruel, it will come from their closest collaborators and from their superiors. The Lord experienced it on the part of the apostles, and they from each other— Peter by Paul (Gal. 2 : 11), and Paul by Barnabas (Acts 15 : 39).

In a word, all of life will be visited by the crucified Lord. This is not tragic; it is the destiny chosen by the Father for his Son and for those whom he wishes to unite with him. But it is important to be aware of it early, lest time be lost in seeking to avoid suffering.

4. The cross visits also *all of our being, to the very depths.* It usually comes to us in a form we should not have chosen. And what a difference there is between this cross and our voluntary mortifications, rightly undertaken, but always prudently stopping short of the limit of our capacity. The cross of the Lord goes beyond mere human strength to the place where we can only cry out in the dark, that is, even to Gethsemane. To know it in advance will at least remind us to cry to him when the time comes.

The cross of the Lord affects the whole being for this very reason, that it is beyond physical or moral strength. The suffering can be at once physical and spiritual, sometimes more of the one than the other; and at such times no medical treatment in the world can shorten the trial.

5. *The cross will always be folly.*

The true cross of the Lord always resembles a failure—a deplorable failure. And when it affects the apostolate, it brings about an apparent delay in the coming of the Kingdom of God. The death of Jesus on the cross apparently compromised his mission to bring the good news. The illness of a religious in the bloom of her youth apparently restricts the effectiveness of the community apostolate. But in the light of Christ's death and resurrection the failure is only apparent, unless she who suffers also fails to accept the cross and carry it with love; then indeed it is a radical failure from every point of view.

The cross will also be folly *for the one who bears it*. For we always bear it badly and often fall beneath its weight. The cross is never carried in triumph, and when a moment of respite comes, no one can ever look back with pride or satisfaction upon what has been accomplished. This must be understood from the beginning of religious life, so that the thought of suffering may never become a source of subtle pride.

The cross is folly also *in the eyes of others*, and perhaps the sufferer will become an object of derision or pity. Some may say, 'Who would have thought it?' 'We expected so much of her.' She will be conscious of this and it will be a source of cruel suffering for her.

She will even have the impression of being *a fool before God*, of being rejected by him. The cross is a 'night', the most terrible of nights, that of the spirit. God has disappeared from the eyes of the soul: 'My God, my God, why hast thou forsaken me?' (Matt. 27:46; Ps. 22:1).

6. The cross of the religious is the cross of the Lord only if from the depths of her agony she *consents willingly* though obscurely to the designs of God. This cannot be achieved all at once. For a long time and on many occasions she will stumble and fall, asking, 'Father, if it be possible . . .', until the day when she is finally able to stammer, 'Thy will be done.' This is an austere doctrine, no doubt; but not inhuman, for it is not beyond the strength of man upheld by God.

Christ willed to experience our human condition with all its sorrows. No doubt he could have saved us otherwise. He could have passed directly into his risen state and from there, encouraged us to hold fast. But he chose to be our companion on the way of the cross. He wanted to experience every form of suffering: poverty, the loss of a dear one (John 11:35), the hatred of enemies, distrust and condemnation on the part of legitimate authority (John 11:51). He willed to undergo the most acute mental anguish even to Gethsemane and Calvary; he chose to pass through terrible physical suffering, to endure his death agony and actually to die. As Saint Paul writes in his Letter to the Hebrews, 'We have not a high priest who is unable to sympathize with our weaknesses, but one who in every respect has been tempted as we are, yet without sinning' (Heb. 4:15). This is why Jesus is always the companion of those who suffer in this world; and they in turn can, if they wish, be with him in his sufferings. He was alone on 7 April of the year 30 on Calvary; today he is no longer alone and will never again be alone, for those whom suffering has touched can say with St Paul, 'I am crucified with Christ'.

In a letter to his brother in which he explained the motives of his conversion to Catholicism, Karl Stern, a German Jew, referred to the Jewish massacres under the Nazi regime:

> The more I meditate on them, on those nightmarish last years, months and hours of their lives, the more I come to believe in Jesus Christ, the Son of the living God. . . . There is something extraordinary in the suffering of Christ. It seems to include all human suffering, and yet it can be 'completed' by the suffering of individual persons. . . . There is only One who unites all these secrets in his suffering, and that is Jesus Christ. The more you dwell on it, the more it becomes clear that in his agony he anticipated the hidden agonies of innumerable individuals. For centuries the Church has meditated on the five Sorrowful Mysteries of the Rosary or on the fourteen Stations of the Cross. And the more people did so, the more the agony of our Lord became revealed. It has innumerable facets. It anticipates, it contains your and my life in a singular way.[1]

7. The cross of the Lord is but a stage on the way leading from death to life. It is *a Pasch*, that is, *a passage*. The cross unites us to Christ in both his death and his resurrection so that we can truly say we have risen with Christ (Col. 3:1). The consecrated religious must cling to this hope, even though it is obscure and painful. When St Paul speaks of the 'Mystery of Christ' (Rom. 16:25), he is referring to his death and resurrection (cf. Rom. 6). This also must be emphatically taught. The Christian life in its baptismal seed is a participation in this mystery: 'We were buried therefore with him by baptism unto death, so that as Christ was raised from the dead by the glory of the Father, we too might walk in

[1] Karl Stern, *Le Buisson Ardent* (Editions du Seuil, Paris). *The Pillar of Fire* (New York: Harcourt Brace, 1951), pp. 288, 294-5.

newness of life' (Rom. 6:4). The religious profession to which the novices are called is not a new baptism (the expression is inaccurate), but a true renewal of baptism in its significance and the graces it brings. All the stages of religious life are present in this profession, with their double phase of death and of life. All the suffering that is to come is included and offered at the religious profession, but the promise of life is also contained in it.

Complete and sensible instruction on this mystery of a consecrated life organically joined to the mystery of the death and resurrection of Jesus, will allow the spirituality of a young sister to find a proper balance by integrating the two traditional tendencies: that which places the accent on death and insists especially on penance, but runs the risk of turning into an austere rigorism; and that which places the accent on the resurrection and insists especially on optimism and joy, but runs the risk of eliminating the mystery and avoiding the cross as a shame and a misfortune.

8. It is thus that young religious will come to understand how a successful apostolate is exercised; not according to results measured exteriorly, but *on the mysterious plane in which life emerges from death,* where hearts are touched by slowly maturing grace purchased at the price of suffering. 'Every branch that does bear fruit he prunes, that it may bear more fruit' (John 15:2). In this clear and accurate understanding of the apostolate that awaits them, young sisters will find their true protection and principle of defence against the activism to which they are exposed.

To allow girls full of good will and many illusions to embrace a life of consecration without teaching them these basic facts in the noviceship is to betray their trust. But if they understand at least in general how they are called to participate in the death and resurrection of Jesus, this knowledge will become a principle of unification in their life and help to light up certain difficult sections along the way.

II. SUPERIORS MUST FOLLOW UP THIS TEACHING IN ORDER THAT RELIGIOUS MAY LEARN TO 'UNDERSTAND' THE CROSS

The young sister leaves the noviceship armed with many principles; she must now rediscover by experience what she has learned in theory. It is for this reason that her first mission is of primary importance, and her first superior will probably have more influence over her than all those previously in charge of her training. Major superiors have a grave duty to select with the greatest care the local superiors whose responsibility it will be to continue the formation of the young religious.

The young sister must now learn to read in the book of life. What will be the nature of her first cross? Exteriorly, it may be insignificant: fear of failure in her new work, difficulty of adaptation to a milieu into which she comes as a stranger, or simply a conflict of character—the cause matters little. What does matter is its repercussions in the sensibility of the young religious. The local superior must always look at the problem from the point of view of the sister, regardless of how insignificant it may seem to her. She must forget all else to enter into the soul of the other and judge the problem there. This is one of the most serious obligations of a superior.

The first suffering in the life of a young sister comes in the form of a 'temptation' in the biblical sense, that is, a trial permitted by God from which the worst may result, but also the best. For the religious it is an occasion of growing in faith from the moment in which she chooses the Lord, now no longer with the rather blind generosity of one who does not know, but with the seriousness of purpose of her who begins to see with new vision, the vision of faith. But before making such a choice, there is a path of suffering to be followed in the dark, along which the young sister needs guidance. She must learn by experience the sense of the text she knows so well: 'Watch and pray, that you may not enter into temptation' (Matt. 26:41). If the superior is there to remind her and pray with her, the passage will be effected more easily.

How many religious flounder because they failed to make this transition. The first suffering was not recognized in the light of faith, and it left in its wake a fund of bitterness and disillusion. The passing years brought their share of difficulties, unforeseen illness, lack of understanding on the part of authority, an unexpected and painful change, exhausting labours, trying temptations, the conflicts of living in community. Each problem left behind it, like an ebbing wave, its residue of rancour and discouragement. At length the depths of the soul were clogged, prayer was stifled, and the religious took refuge in the automatism of gestures and the mediocrity of spiritual ambitions.

Annual retreats do not awaken them; it is as though the mainspring of their life had been broken. Why this failure to fulfil a religious vocation that started out full of desires and good will? Doubtless because they met no one, either superior or confessor, who was able to impart to them an 'understanding' of the cross.

Or perhaps they were told too quickly and tactlessly; they were not given time to weep. It is so easy for a superior who has not entered into the heart of a religious to become impatient before an emotional reaction, and confront her with the argument of the cross that she should carry and the spirit of faith that she should have.

Let superiors read the Gospels and study the humility and the patience of Christ. In the incident of the disciples on their way to Emmaus, for example (Luke 24:13-35), he respects the normal details of psychological maturation, and practises that pastoral charity which may be summed up in two complementary attitudes: the art of asking questions, and the art of listening to the answers. He does not upbraid them before asking the simplest of questions, 'What things?' and allowing them fully to unburden their hearts while he listens.

The lesson is of immense importance for those who have the responsibility for consecrated religious and must help them to understand the cross in their life. They must give them time to suffer, to express their suffering, time to weep if need be, and if necessary, they must weep and suffer with them. Only after this necessary stage has been passed can the superior speak of the demands of Christ's cross and hope to be heard.

'O foolish men . . . Was it not necessary that the Christ should suffer these things and enter into his glory?' Christ *had to* pass through death to arrive at the resurrection. The Gospel message must not be devalued by human explanations. If, for example, a sister is suffering because of an unexpected transfer, superiors must not justify the measure by giving earthly reasons, saying that the good of the Congregation necessitated such a move, that it was not possible to act otherwise. The works of men alone depend upon such arguments. To teach their subjects to interpret their lives with an understanding of the cross is one of the most beautiful tasks of superiors. Events which bring sorrow do indeed have human causes, human beings with their qualities and especially their defects, and they do have a human explanation. It is unfortunately possible to see nothing beyond this

151

human view. But these events also take place on a divine plane involving the three divine Persons, and they have an explanation in the mind of God.

To 'understand' the cross is to be able to discern this divine plan in all the sorrows of life. Those who have been taught to do so possess the key which will prove to be the unifying principle of their whole life.

Is this asking too much of superiors? How can they become educators of this calibre? First, they must have suffered themselves, and they especially must possess the key which will permit them henceforth to look at suffering with divine vision.

If they have suffered, and if in their suffering they have clung with their whole being to the Lord's will, they will not devaluate the message. They have understood the cross, but not immediately. They adhered to the person of the Lord before understanding, and gradually the light came. They are then able gently to teach others (they know from experience that they must not go too quickly).

If they have really suffered, they will speak with *humility*. It is easy to encourage others boldly when one has not suffered. Those who really know the cross and how badly it can be carried will speak of it with moderation, humility, and even trembling.

But they will speak with *firmness*, refusing to compromise, and with *optimism*. They should not blame those religious who may have disappointed them. Which of us is not each day a disappointment to the Lord?

Finally, they will speak with *hope*. There is never a Good Friday without an Easter Sunday. But here again, they must express themselves very carefully; it is a matter for supernatural hope which has nothing to do with human hope. The latter may be described in this way: 'You feel badly today,

but never mind, you'll feel better tomorrow.' Our hope does
not consist in anticipating a cessation of suffering; it is to be
found within the sorrow itself. 'Your sorrow will turn into
joy' (John 16:20).

Such an understanding will permit religious better than
anyone else to understand the suffering of the world. People
frequently confide in religious; when the latter are well
acquainted with the human milieu in which they labour,
they are able to discern the suffering concealed behind each
door or each face. Let them gather these fragments of the
true cross dispersed throughout the world and offer them
in their daily Mass. If the occasion presents itself, they may
even be able to open the eyes of those whom they meet to
the true dimensions of the mystery into which they themselves have resolutely entered.

Catherine de Hueck, that 'Christian among the poor',
writes in her letters to religious:

> Life is not easy. . . . His cross was hard. It was made
> of green, rough wood. It was unplaned and full of splin-
> ters, small and large. You deliberately chose to lie on it! ...
> But here you are asked to do more. You are being asked
> to lift this sign of salvation before the clear eyes of youth
> and explain to them that, if they want happiness, peace,
> and joy that surpasses all understanding, they too must lie
> on the cross. They must lie on it because they are in love
> with him who first hung upon it in utter desolation and
> agony for love of them.[1]

---

[1] Quoted in *Informations Catholiques Internationales*, 1 Feb. 1960,
p. 3. Catherine de Hueck, *Dear Sister* (Milwaukee: Bruce, 1953)
pp. 50-1.

III

Formation of Superiors in the Exercise of Authority

A father should be loved . . . and not feared. . . . They will consider you as a leader if you are as a simple soldier with them. Be in their midst as one of them, and they will single you out among many. Freedom rebels under oppression. No one obtains more from a free man than he who avoids treating him as a slave . . .

Saint Jerome to the Bishop Theophilus

THERE IS much discussion today on the subject of obedience and with reason, for obedience is one of the bulwarks of a consecrated life; and where it does not exist, or is poorly understood or imperfectly lived, there is only a caricature of religious life.

An excellent work on obedience has been published in the present series.[1] It is not necessary to repeat what has already been written there. Other books and articles of unequal value are appearing regularly on the same subject.

Much less has been written, however, about the exercise of authority. This is understandable, for the subject is more difficult. Authority is not merely a function, it is also a virtue. In reality, obedience and authority are complementary aspects of the same virtue. It is therefore psychologically necessary to have long obeyed in order to be able to command (and it is well to return to obedience for a time before assuming once more the direction of a community). From a spiritual angle it is necessary to have experienced and pondered in prayer the mystical value of obedience as Christ lived it, in order to be able to exercise authority in the spirit of Jesus.

[1] *L'obéissance*, Coll. 'Problèmes de la Religieuse d'Aujourd'hui' (Paris: Editions du Cerf, 1951). *Obedience*, Rel. Life Series, III (London: Blackfriars, 1953).

This is not sufficiently understood; and although there is often question of the formation of sisters in obedience, the problem of the formation of superiors in the art of commanding is neglected, in spite of the laudable efforts in this direction made by certain forward-looking Congregations, and institutes held under the auspices of federations of major superiors.

Pius XII often insisted on the importance of the role of superiors and the necessity of training them. On 15 September 1952 he said to the superiors general gathered in Rome:

> It is no doubt true, as psychology affirms, that the woman invested with authority does not succeed as easily as a man in finding the exact formula for combining strictness with kindness and establishing the balance between them. That is an added reason for cultivating your motherly sentiments. You can, of course, say that the vows have exacted from your sisters, as from yourselves, a great sacrifice. They have renounced their family, the happiness of marriage and the intimacy of the home. It is a sacrifice of great value, of decisive importance for the apostolate of the Church, but it is still a sacrifice. Those of your sisters whose souls are noblest and the most refined are the ones who feel this detachment most keenly. . . . The religious Order must take the place of the family, as far as possible, and it is you, the superiors general, who are expected in the first instance to breathe the warmth of family affection into the community life of the sisters.[1]

It is the more surprising that so little concern is shown for the education and formation of superiors, as it is much more difficult to command than to obey, especially to command well, seeking the divine will and respecting the personal dignity of subordinates.

[1] Courtois, *op. cit.*, No. 479, p. 217.

Certain human qualities are indeed necessary, and if some are lacking nothing can be done about it, formation sessions notwithstanding. Supernatural virtues are also needed, and higher superiors must exert a constant effort to develop these in local superiors; the Church, for her part, will need to exercise great vigilance towards higher superiors.

The development of consecrated vocations according to God's plan is closely dependent upon the holiness and the educational skill of superiors.

Three precise examples have been used—that of prayer, of fraternal charity, and of understanding the cross—to show that the formation of a religious cannot be limited to the novitiate but must be continued throughout her entire life. What qualities then will be required in a superior, to make her a master of the spiritual life of her sisters. so that she may foster their development at every stage of their life. If it is true that the demands made on contemporary religious require a continual and careful training on the part of those responsible, what shall be said of the need to train superiors for this task?

The exercise of power is dangerous by its very nature; it flatters the tendencies of original self-love too much not to corrupt little by little the superiors who are not clear sighted and vigilant. The danger is all the more serious as there is no question here of merely human authority demanding only external obedience and leaving the conscience free to protest, if need be. Religious authority is a true participation in divine authority and subjects know it well, since they bind themselves not only exteriorly but interiorly as well. To such obedience corresponds an authority far more absolute, since it is binding upon conscience itself.

In this part of my book I propose in the first place briefly to outline a biblical theology of authority. Then I shall try to describe the psychological and institutional limitations to the exercise of power. Finally, I shall attempt to draw up the principal phases of a plan for the education of superiors.

9

Christ, Shepherd and Servant

I will set up over them one shepherd, my servant David, and
he shall feed them.

Ezek. 34:23

THE BEST way to understand the greatness of a superior's
task and measure its demands is by reading the book of the
word of God. The principle of all authority resides in God.
The Bible is not made up of an accumulation of abstract
theories. It is a living book in which God confronts man in
person, and not only reveals himself to him, but assumes the
precise attitudes which he wishes him to adopt as his own.
The Old Testament is God's meeting-place with man; there
he speaks to him and teaches him by a definite method
which modern educators would term 'objective'. As if this
were not sufficiently clear, God revealed himself even closer
to man by becoming incarnate, and the New Testament is
the place where Jesus, by living his life in the presence of his
disciples and by instructing them, educated those also who
would later exercise in his name a portion of his authority
in the Church.

To say that the superior holds the place of God is to assert
a fact of capital importance, rooted not only in the Bible,
but in all of spiritual tradition. The obedience of religious in
faith is wholly founded on this truth upon which we can

161

never insist enough, provided it is done with respect for the human person.

But if superiors themselves become convinced of this in prayer and humility, they will also discover how very much God expects of them in their exercise of authority. For this authority has its source and its model in the sovereignty of the heavenly Father communicated by him to the Word incarnate, exercised by Jesus, and finally delegated by him to the Church and within the Church.

I. SHEPHERD AND SERVANT

These two key-words found in biblical themes of great importance cast a penetrating light on the character of the Father's sovereignty as exercised by Christ.

1. *God reveals himself constantly as the Shepherd.*

It is difficult for us in our modern civilization to realize the deep significance of the word shepherd, which to the Jews was so full of the strength and warmth of human experience. The words shepherd, flock, sheep and lamb, were powerfully evocative in the context of their life.

The authors of the Psalms address God as shepherd:

Give ear, O Shepherd of Israel,
   thou who leadest Joseph like a flock! (Ps. 80:1)

For he is our God,
   and we are the people of his pasture,
   and the sheep of his hand. (Ps. 95:7)

The Lord is my Shepherd, I shall not want;
   he makes me lie down in green pastures.

He leads me beside still waters;
　　he restores my soul. . . .
I fear no evil, for thou art with me;
　　thy rod and thy staff, they comfort me. (Ps. 23 : 1-2, 4)

To represent God, the prophets multiply images borrowed
from pastoral life.

He will feed his flock like a shepherd,
　　he will gather the lambs in his arms,
he will carry them in his bosom,
　　and gently lead those that are with young. (Is. 40 : 11)

Ezekiel is even more explicit in the celebrated chapter that
inspired the New Testament allegory of the Good Shepherd
and the parable of the Good Samaritan :

For thus says the Lord God : Behold, I, I myself will
search for my sheep, and will seek them out. As a shepherd seeks out his flock when some of his sheep have been
scattered abroad, so will I seek out my sheep . . . and I
will feed them on the mountains of Israel, by the foun-
tains, and in all the inhabited places of the country. . . .
I myself will be the shepherd of my sheep, and I will make
them lie down. . . .　(Ezek. 34 : 11-15)

And the prophet shows Yahweh the Shepherd at work in
the most diverse attitudes, all inspired by his profound concern for the sheep : he strengthens the weak, cares for the
sick, seeks the lost sheep and brings it back to the fold, dis-
tributes suitable food; nor does he forget the healthy—he
protects them from extortion, leads them to rest, prevents
discord among them, etc. 'And you are my sheep, the sheep
of my pasture, and I am your God' (Ezek. 34 : 31).

But soon the name shepherd begins to designate not only

Yahweh, but also him whom he will send, so that it became one of the names proper to the Messiah.

In the same chapter in which God reveals himself as a shepherd attentive to his flock, Ezekiel continues: 'I will set up over them one shepherd, my servant David, and he shall feed them: he shall feed them and be their shepherd' (Ezek. 34:23).

But it is in the New Testament especially that the Messiah reveals himself as the Shepherd. The allegory of the shepherd (John 10) and the parable of the lost sheep (Luke 15:3-7) are very familiar, so familiar that the full import of their teaching escapes our comprehension. We must read and reread them in order to discover all the nuances of the love of Jesus our Shepherd for us, his sheep. He places them on the right road, then walks before them; yet more, he is himself the way. He enters by the door of the sheep-fold; more, he is the door through which they pass to be saved. He gives them their food and communicates life to them, eternal life. He even lays down his own life for his sheep. He knows his sheep by name, and they know him. He leaves all to seek the one that is lost, and when he has found it and placed it on his shoulders, he has more joy at the thought of this one than for all the others that caused him no worry.

The apostles spoke of their master as Shepherd and considered all authority in the Church as a participation in the pastoral charge of Jesus. Peter thus exhorts the presbyters: 'Tend the flock of God that is your charge, not by constraint but willingly . . . not as domineering over those in your charge but being examples to the flock. And when the chief Shepherd is manifested you will obtain the unfading crown of glory' (I Peter 5:2-4).

2. The other name proper to Jesus which defines the nature of his authority is that of *Servant*.

If he is a shepherd, it is because the Father has confided the sheep to him; but towards the Father he considers himself only an obedient servant.

The entire Bible affirms very strongly that God alone possesses authority, and that all those who exercise it in his name are called servants (a very strong word; in Hebrew it signifies 'slave'). So it is concerning Moses (Josh. 1:2; Deut. 34:5), Joshua (Josh. 24:29), the prophets (2 Kings 17:23; Jer. 7:25), David (Ps. 17:1; 89:4; 89:21).

To Christ, the name Servant is more essential than that of Shepherd. He is Shepherd of his disciples only because the Father has 'given' them to him (John 17:2; 17:6; 17:9; 17:11; 17:12; 17:24). But the name and function of Servant are essential to Jesus. The Servant whom Isaiah and the Psalms frequently announce (Is. 42:1-4; 49:3-6; 50:1-10; 52:13 to 53:12; Ps. 116, esp. v. 16; Ps. 119) is led by the Holy Spirit; he is gentle, yet filled with the strength of God; completely submissive to God, he is ready to suffer and lose all things, relying on divine help alone.

Jesus is the Servant who was foretold: 'I am among you as one who serves' (Luke 22:27). 'The Son of man came not to be served but to serve, and to give his life as a ransom for many' (Matt. 20:28; Mark 10:45). At the moment when he is about to wash the feet of his disciples, his clothing is that of a slave and he performs the office of a slave. But at the same time he reminds them that he is the Lord: 'You call me Teacher and Lord; and you are right, for so I am' (John 13:13). It is as Lord and Master that he washes the feet of his disciples. His authority places him at the service not only of the Father, but also of the apostles whom he governs and educates. And at the moment when he is about to found his Church and delegate to his disciples the authority he received from his Father, he says explicitly that this unexpected gesture must henceforth be the inspiration of all who will possess any power in the Church. 'If I then, your Lord and Teacher, have washed your feet, you also ought to wash one another's feet. For I have given you an example, that you also should do as I have done to you' (John 13 : 14).

The name of Servant truly describes the mission of Jesus, that is, his attitude towards his Father and towards his disciples. He is *at the same time* the Servant of God and that of his brothers. He lives in contemplation before God whose name is always on his lips because his heart is full of love for him. His food is to do the will of him who sent him (John 4 : 34). He always does 'what is pleasing to him' (John 8 : 29). It is because he loves the Father that he does as the Father has commanded him (John 14 : 31). And it is because he is totally subject to the Father that he is at the service of others, in the midst of them as one who serves. Even when he commands or decides, there is never in him the least trace of a spirit of superiority. Submission to his Father fills so completely the field of his consciousness that there is no room for any sentiment in him but a desire to serve; and the service of the Father is so much a part of his very being that it includes and incorporates the service of others. It is all one and the same service.

II. AUTHORITY IS EXERCISED IN DEPENDENCE ON CHRIST SHEPHERD AND SERVANT

A superior is united with Christ in many ways: as a Christian through her baptism, as a religious through her profession which is a renewal of her baptism, and as a superior through the duties entrusted to her, which enable her to participate in the mystery of Christ Shepherd and Servant. Like Christ, she must abide in contemplation before God and seek his fatherly will. No local superior is autonomous, notwithstanding the relative freedom from restraint permitted by higher superiors. Daily to seek the will of God is a terribly exacting programme, and she who possesses authority over her sisters will increase her faith by daily meditation on this subject.

When faced with any particular problem or situation, let her always ask herself, 'What does God wish me to command or advise?' In some cases he may wish her to do nothing. For this reason the superior should often advise rather than command, thus acting on the principle that she has no right to bind souls more than God himself binds them. It is here she will find the courage and self-denial necessary to allow her subordinates to assume initiative.

Then let the superior always ask herself concerning each of her subjects, 'What does the fatherly love of God expect of her?' The will of God which the superior must discover and express is always a form of love. God is a simple being; in him, willing and loving are one and the same act. It is because of sin that we are able to love and desire anything without reference to God. What is more, they who wield authority, whether legitimate or not, have the power of making others act without reference to God. The superior must therefore aim at willing and commanding nothing but in the love of the Father and of her sisters. If she must punish, let it never be done without love and humility, for an immense love is needed to dare inflict even a slight punishment.

Since the will of God, full of love for men, always intends the spiritual growth of souls, the superior must see to this increase with patience, longanimity, hope, and encouragement. She must constantly reflect on the many expressions of Christ's character as Shepherd and Servant, and use them as norms of action for herself. It is impossible to enter into detail; a book would hardly be sufficient.

Let us only take a few instances. What is the pasture to which, after the example of the Good Shepherd, she must lead her sheep? Is it not that of divine life? But she will not be able to guide her sisters to it unless she knows the way. She must know by experience what food they need. 'If I speak in the tongues of men and of angels, but have not love, I am a noisy gong or a clanging cymbal' (I Cor. 13:1).

Let her also think of the lost sheep of which Yahweh and Jesus speak with such tenderness (Ezek. 34:18; Luke 15:4-7). It sometimes happens in a community that one of the sheep is in danger of being lost or has actually gone astray. A superior must then have, not the heart of a judge or a pharisee secure in her power and her peace of conscience, but rather the heart and patience of the Shepherd and the humility of the Servant.

If she is the servant of God after the example of Christ, hers will not be a personal point of view, but that of God in the sense that she will not easily believe her own lights come from God. She 'seeks' this fatherly will of God, and is not afraid to lose face because she needs time to seek. Did not Jesus himself 'seek' the will of his Father? (John 5:30). This need of seeking will prompt her to ask advice, thus guarding her against repulsive absolutism. If she thus seeks the will of God, she will find out that God never constrains souls, but rather solicits them, guides them, calls and helps them—with firmness, yes, but also with flexibility. God has plenty of time; he invented time, so to speak, in order that souls might be educated and enabled gradually to progress. He is ingenious enough to guide each soul along her own personal way; the superior who seeks the will of God will respect this individuality and will not try to make all the sisters pass through the same gate and march in step like soldiers.

If she is the servant of God, she is also, like Jesus, the servant of others. She must be in the midst of her sisters as one who serves; for this reason, before speaking to one of them and giving her an order, above all before administering a rebuke, she will place herself in spirit at her feet like Jesus at the feet of his disciples.

She will then treat her subordinates as adults, not making children of them. She will respect these women who are 'given' to her and who, if they had married, would in spite of their defects, now be the advisers of their husbands and the guides of their children.

In a word, she will command in such a way as to make them love obedience. For obedience cannot be imposed from without; it grows first of all in the depths of the heart, and to teach such obedience requires an habitual contemplation of God and an immense respect for others. But this subject will be taken up later.

III. THE AUTHORITY OF THE SUPERIOR IS EXERCISED WITHIN THE CHURCH AND ON BEHALF OF THE CHURCH

It is true that the early fathers of the desert had no other authority over the disciples who placed themselves under their direction than that which their personal sanctity and experience gave them.

But it is quite otherwise in a religious community. Every religious Congregation has been erected by the Church. Making use of her authority as spouse of Christ, the Church approved the constitutions. Thus the authority of superiors comes only from the Church and can be exercised only within the limits defined by the Church, that is, within the limits of the constitutions. In the large area not covered by the constitutions, the superior may guide, advise, ask, but she cannot command. She will give orders with all the more prudence and discretion as she is more faithful to the constitutions.

Let us add that the responsibility of a superior should not consist merely in promoting regular observance. Observance is not an end in itself; it is only a means. The end towards which a superior should tend with all her energy is the sanctification of each religious and the apostolic activity of the community. In order to attain such an end, commands are not sufficient and are even inadequate; the persuasive force of example is needed. Authority is not merely a matter of commanding and directing; it is especially the power or rather the duty of promoting growth.[1] It is for this reason that authority comes from the Church and is exercised within the Church, for the growth of souls and the efficacy of the apostolate are works of grace which are due to the Church.

Moreover, a community of religious is a figure of the Church (although a sketchy and incomplete one), and the greatness of a superior's function comes from the fact that she holds the trust and the responsibility for this figure of the Church. This is why the unity of the religious in fraternal charity is so important, for this unity alone is able to bear witness and evangelize the world (cf. John 17:21, 23). It is the duty of a superior not only to guide separate individuals, but also to create a family, a happy family. Collective prayer, work, and recreation in common are very important; and when religious living under the same roof never have the opportunity of praying and recreating together or of sharing apostolic experiences, they soon become slaves of their original individualism.

[1] This is the etymological sense of 'auctoritas', which comes from the verb 'augere', to augment.

It is also *for the good of the Church* that the superior exercises authority. When a community is no longer useful to the Church, it is dying, though it may keep up appearances. It is the superior's responsibility to see that her entire community fulfills the mission it has received for the good of the Church. I shall return to this subject in the following chapter. It may merely be recalled here that a religious community is ordered to the glory of God and the good of the Church, and that a superior receives authority for this purpose. The authority does not belong to her and she must not be attached to it. She must peacefully accept being removed from office, should higher superiors judge this to be for the good of the Church. All authority in the Church, even the highest, is never anything else than a service. Jesus said:

You know that the rulers of the Gentiles lord it over them, and their great men exercise authority over them. It shall not be so among you; but whoever would be great among you must be your servant, and whoever would be the first among you must be your slave; even as the Son of man came not to be served but to serve, and to give his life . . . (Matt. 20:25-8)

10

Human Weaknesses in the Exercise of Authority

Fathers, do not provoke your children, lest they become discouraged. . . . You are serving the Lord Christ.

Col. 3:21, 24

WE HAVE seen that authentic obedience alone, after the example of Christ and according to the spirit of the Church, can result in an authentic religious life.

But there is a very close connection between obedience and authority, and religious will advance in the spirit of obedience to the extent that superiors promote a wholesome love for obedience. Here again, religious formation is not limited to the novitiate, and a sister who has the good fortune of living under superiors who are competent educators will each year increase in this 'blessing of obedience'[1] and, at the same time, in conformity to Christ obedient unto death.

There are many obstacles to the practice of obedience on the part of religious, and often these obstacles derive from the same psychological causes as the difficulties of superiors in the exercise of authority.

Modern psychology defines a human being as one affected

[1] Rule of Saint Benedict.

172

by his relations with others: in order to live and thrive, he needs to love and be loved. This confirms what we know of Christian revelation, namely, that it does not merely consist in a set of ethical principles, but that it is also a religion, that is, a relationship between the human person and the divine Persons, and by the same token a mutual interrelationship of human persons among themselves. This is why the Christian revelation is the religion of love.

Mere commands bearing no relation to love are the cause of a child's first difficulties with people. The same phenomenon frequently occurs in religious life without the superior's being necessarily at fault, for it can be caused by the over-passivity of immature subjects. But if precepts and 'points of fidelity' are multiplied as obediences, especially if these bear on the details of daily living; in a word, if such legislation and control are not inspired and justified by love, there is a danger that the sisters will remain in a state of infantilism, or return to it.

There is always a danger in receiving into the noviceship postulants who are psychologically immature. But today there is an added risk. No doubt candidates are often more adult than formerly, having learned to assume professional or apostolic responsibility before entering religion. But none is without psychic flaws and they are no exception. When they are faced with an over-rigid discipline or weakness in authority, they will suffer and their psychic deficiencies will come to the surface. They will either react passively, with vague regret for the lost enrichments of their adulthood; or they will become aggressive.

The superior's manner of exercising authority is extremely important, for she has the power of promoting not only spiritual growth, but that of the entire person—body, mind and soul. Her orders should elicit from her sisters not a passive submission, but the total engagement of their liberty, after the example of the Father who obtained from Christ the free gift of himself: 'For this reason the Father loves me, because I lay down my life . . . No one takes it from me, but I lay it down of my own accord. I have the power to lay it down, and I have the power to take it again: this charge I have received from my Father' (John 10:17-8).

The number of good and excellent superiors in religious Congregations proves that the observations set forth in this chapter do not apply to all; nevertheless, as Pius XII said to the superiors general, 15 September 1952, 'it is no doubt true, as psychology affirms, that the woman invested with authority does not succeed as easily as a man in finding the exact formula for combining strictness with kindness and establishing the balance between them.'[1]

What are these psychological obstacles and difficulties encountered by superiors and subjects, which prevent a successful formation in obedience?

I. AUTHORITARIANISM

It is not necessary to define the term, for everyone has met an authoritarian person. Anyone who exercises power of any kind has a natural tendency to accentuate it by an attitude, a tone of voice, a gesture, etc. Authoritarianism, however, may have very diverse causes.

1. It may come from a certain timidity, never acknowledged but present since childhood.

The timid superior will hesitate to give a merited rebuke, for *she is afraid to confront an adult*, even when this adult is her subordinate. She prefers to wait, hoping that the reason for the rebuke will disappear. But meanwhile the cause

[1] Courtois, *op. cit.*, No. 479, p. 217.

remains in her mind and upon it accumulate other complaints against the sister. One day the 'last straw' is laid, or perhaps she is particularly tired, and she makes a scene out of all proportion to the actual cause of her annoyance.

Perhaps again she cannot fully accept having to command others because she suffers from an inferiority complex of which she cannot rid herself. Thus her authority seems to her to be always in danger; every younger sister who comes to her house appears more gifted and better trained than she is. She experiences an instinctive need to compensate for her feeling of inferiority by imposing her authority more strictly.

Or else this superior, who has so little self-confidence and distrusts almost all the sisters, will seek out the weaker ones who, through affection or false virtue, will always agree with her. Yet it is a sign of adult psychology to be able to receive with calmness and gratitude an opinion that differs from one's own. But the timid superior is not fully an adult and avoids all conflicts with persons who stand on their own feet.

This superior may also protect herself by projecting her emotions around her as a defence mechanism against opinions that differ from her own. She grieves and shows her grief, especially in matters of slight importance, and in this way she enslaves and binds her sisters.

These various examples proceed from the same psychological immaturity. Is it necessary to add that the superior's immaturity engenders or maintains the same immaturity in her subjects? Far from educating her sisters both humanly and spiritually, she develops in them, either by contact or by reaction, attitudes inspired by the same infantilism. An authoritarian superior will incite in her subjects either aggressiveness against all authority, or a silence that will isolate and protect them against the superior's personality. The same attitude is found in adolescent girls whose parents are too strict.

2. The authoritarian character of certain superiors may also be the natural result of *a taste for power*.

This type of person has probably begun to impose her will on others long before entering the convent. As a superior, she shows herself meticulous and tyrannical, a sentinel who desires to know everything in detail even to the very thoughts of her subjects. She organizes everything herself and will not tolerate any initiative from others, even in areas in which she has no competence and where obedience does not come into play.

The seriousness of this situation lies in the fact that obedience itself is invoked to bring about the subjugation of souls. Such a superior is incapable of distinguishing between essentials and accidentals. All is important; everything is a matter for obedience, and this is how 'points of fidelity' are multiplied. Religious need enlightenment to be able to distinguish between the area in which obedience must be freely and wholeheartedly given, and that in which the Church allows freedom of thought.

Such a superior demands universal obedience, not to God, but to her own will from which nothing escapes. Obedience becomes an end in itself, without reference to love, and from this come many misinterpretations of obedience. Young sisters trained by such superiors must obey at any cost, so as to break their self-will. Sisters are scolded, even in public, like children. Abject fear, degrading and depressing, is infused into them.

There is no impulse Godward because they have lost their human dignity; their relations with others are lifeless, without vigour and without initiative, and such passivity sterilizes their activity because it inspires contempt.

Should the community include personalities strong enough to resist such treatment, the superior will divide her subjects into two groups. She will lean upon the most infantile of her sisters in order to isolate the others. Weak souls have a natural inclination to curry favour with those in power; she will make use of this weakness to exact confidences and tales concerning the others.

What will be the consequences of such an attitude on the part of the superior? The best religious, those who are humanly well balanced and totally dedicated to the Lord, will find therein their daily cross and a means of increasing their love. 'We know that in everything God works for good with those who love him' (Rom. 8:28). But if subjects can live their obedience in the mystery of a spiritual night, this does not justify the arbitrary exercise of authority on the part of superiors. The other sisters endowed with an equally strong personality but with less virtue, will rebel and grow bitter, and they will find their only refuge in silence. The rest will submit, that is, will give up thinking and acting for themselves to become simple executants, and if the efface-ment to which they are condemned corresponds to a natural passivity, they will be satisfied with such an existence and will lose their human dignity, even in the eyes of lay people.

All these forms of authoritarianism are, then, the conse-quences of stunted affective development. Such persons are incapable of truly loving God with a love that completely takes possession of the entire being—body, soul, and mind. Neither can they love others, for on the way they encounter the obstacle of self-love, self-seeking, in a word, selfishness in all its forms. There is a quality and an intensity of love for God and the neighbour which only persons with a fully matured affectivity can attain.

II. MATERNALISM

The word—if we may be allowed this neologism—refers to a deviation from the motherly sentiments which a superior should have towards the religious of her community. The superior must indeed act as a mother towards her sisters, with all the warmth of affection, the devotedness and the self-forgetfulness of a true mother towards her adult children.

But it sometimes happens that a superior will try to safeguard her authority not by harsh measures, but by means of a skilful hold on the affection of her sisters. She desires to create a family spirit, which is very praiseworthy; but in doing so she reduces her sisters to the status of children and takes them back to the days when nothing else was required of them than docility and affection.

Maternalism is perhaps more stealthily effective than authoritarianism in maintaining the sisters in a state of immaturity. For authoritarianism produces in gifted subjects either a defence reaction or, in the more virtuous, spiritual progress through the acceptance of suffering. But maternalism leaves subjects without defence. How, by what means, and in the name of what principles, will they protect themselves against an authority which, far from being too severe, is covered with a cloak of kindness and gentleness?

Yet they sense in an obscure way that their liberty is being stifled by the development of affective elements to the detriment of those which are rational and willed. It is not easy for a superior to make an exact distinction between legitimate authority and motherly thoughtfulness on one hand, and an all-possessive proliferation of the emotions and the annexation of hearts on the other. Nor is it easy for a subject to distinguish between obedience and legitimate filial affection,

178

and a return to the passivity and complete dependence of the unborn child.

In a community of sisters thus formed or deformed, everything depends upon the will of the superior. The superior is consulted about every detail; the sisters seem incapable of having an opinion of their own. They are not unhappy under such an administration; on the contrary, they experience a great deal of satisfaction, but an unwholesome satisfaction, a kind of cowardly enjoyment. A group which has basked several years in this warm atmosphere becomes ungovernable under another superior; for all new authority, no matter how well balanced, will always seem too harsh. And sisters who have known the turbid pleasure of a child's submission under the spell of an affectionate superior, are almost incapable of recovering a human stature.

III. THE RIGIDITY OF HABIT

A new superior endowed with good judgement and humility is usually well aware of the dangers and deviations that threaten her. But the most subtle danger is that of habit, for it acts very slowly, almost stealthily, and it is so subtle and impalpable that the victim of habit is the only one not to notice it.

Certain established rules of the religious life render it doubly easy to get into a rut; these have such force that the human element is easily sacrificed to them, whereas in the plan of God the rules should be at the service of individuals, to help them come to him. A few examples will suffice.

1. *The ritualism of obedience.*

An order given by a superior to a sister should normally have been pondered in prayer, so that it may in fact be the expression of the divine will, sought and recognized by the superior. Likewise the obedience of a subject is a sensible sign of her dependence on God. When love of God is no longer perceived as the source of authority and the foundation of obedience, habit comes in to harden or degrade the command, and ritualism, to fossilize submission. One major superior wrote to her local superiors: 'In our convents a certain deportment, certain acts, are habitually imposed without any attempt to obtain agreement at the deepest level of the heart and will of subjects. The sisters thus become guarded and passive, if not antagonistic. In grave matters they may be forced to submit, but a latent revolt remains at the bottom of their heart.' 'The Rule is not an aid to sanctity; it becomes corrupted by being lowered to the level of mere regulations, and there is neither conversion, true commitment, nor response to the exigencies of the Gospel.'

This point of view is very accurate. The Rule, the holy Rule, should educate the sisters in the liberty of the children of God. When it descends to the rank of mere regulations, it enters into the most insignificant details, determines attitudes and exterior deportment, gestures, the direction of one's glance, the position of the hands, the manner of walking, etc. Then it is that the Rule minimized to regulations dehumanizes the religious and reduces her to the state of a robot.

2. Marks of respect

It is normal that a superior should be respected as a mother is respected by her children. It is less normal, especially in our time, that such marks of respect be lavished upon her as they were upon sovereigns of past ages. The superior should be freed from mythical notions that surround her, and come down from the Olympus on which certain traditions would maintain her. These external marks of respect come from two sources: either from the Middle Ages (in some Congregations sisters still kneel before the superior as vassals formerly knelt before their sovereign); or they come from the customs of the nineteenth-century middle class; on these customs the religious deportment of certain Congregations (especially in France) has been modelled.

Young postulants may accept these usages, but they do not understand them. Besides, superiors worthy of the office find it difficult to receive such marks of deference, nor do they need them to obtain respect and obedience.

To ask for greater simplicity would not be yielding to the influence of a worldly spirit. Are not these very customs, on the contrary, themselves indications of such a spirit?

3. *Permanence of superiorships*

Someone has said pleasantly, 'The main requirement for a superior is that she should already have been one.' It must be recognized that in many Congregations a local superior will remain so, even if she moves from one house to another, until the age of retirement and even after.

It is contrary to the spirit of Canon Law (c. 505) to maintain a superior in the same house for more than six years. But it is contrary to the religious spirit and to simple wisdom to maintain a local superior at the head of several houses successively without from time to time imposing upon her a period of obedience in the ranks. Moreover, it would be an excellent practice for a superior going out of office to remain in the same house.

Let it not be said that too few sisters are capable of being made superiors. No doubt this is true if as many superiors are needed as there are missions of four, three, and even two sisters. But why tolerate the existence of such small communities?

The argument of the scarcity of subjects capable of directing a religious house is a dull one, and if Congregations were more daring, they would certainly find more superiors than they think. Besides, the prospect of returning to the ranks in six years would have a sobering effect and provide a wholesome protection against deviations caused by habit. It is important that a newly-appointed superior should 'understand that a superiorship is a burden rather than an honour, a service confided to her for a time, of which she will probably be relieved in a few years. She must understand from the start that she has not been appointed superior for life, so that when she is relieved of office, she may humbly accept it as normal once again to assume her place among her sisters.'[1] The superiors general gathered in Congress at Rome in 1952 expressed the following wish :

> For the formation and continued development of superiors . . . young religious should not be excluded from higher office if they have the necessary natural and spiritual qualifications. Care must be taken not to ask more than Canon Law exacts, nor should we be obstinate in the question of re-election. It is the mind of the Church that her laws and the constitutions of the institute be observed (both of which prescribe the change of superiors) so that no religious superior may be deprived of the blessing of obedience. It is to be noted that when conditions are equal between a superior in office and a new candidate, preference should be given to the new candidate. In this way unpleasant situations can be avoided and at the same time a greater number of religious will be formed for governing.[2]

The problem is somewhat different when it is question of

[1] *Bulletin de l'Union des Supérieures Majeures*, No. 8, Nov. 1958, p. 12.
[2] Sacra Congregatio de Religiosis, *Acta et Documenta Congressus Internationalis Superiorissarum Generalium*, 1952, p. 302.

a superior general and her council. These officials are not normally elected for life. Nevertheless in very large Congregations a superior general must remain in office for a long period of time, namely twelve years and even longer. The larger the Congregation, the longer it takes her to become familiar with the various groups.[1]

This permanence is not so necessary for her councillors. Let them be changed as often as possible, not only so that new blood may circulate in the council, but in order to avoid the formation of a caste, a sort of coral reef whose various elements, closely soldered together, finally constitute an insuperable barrier.

It is also advisable that an out-going superior general should not become a member of the general council (at least for one year), in order that her successor may have full liberty of action.

We must keep wide awake and not allow ourselves to be

---

[1] The re-election of a superior general after twelve years of government should be very closely supervised by the bishop of the diocese in which the chapter is held. Cardinal Larraona, then Secretary of the Sacred Congregation of Religious, said to the superiors general at the Congress in Rome in 1952:

The S. Congregation is not only not favourable to election beyond the terms provided in the constitutions, but it is opposed to it on principle. Superiors and capitulars should remember that they, no less than their subjects, have an obligation to observe the law of the Church. Perpetuation of individuals in office tends to prevent the formation of capable superiors, or makes it necessary for them to be chosen from within a closed circle. . . . In case of a superior general, this re-election is called postulation. . . . The fact of having the two-thirds majority must be accompanied with sufficiently serious reasons to influence the judgement of the S. Congregation. The reasons will be judged with severity, and the confirmation of re-election after the term fixed by the constitutions will constitute a rare exception. (Sacra Congregatio de Religiosis, *Acta et Documenta Congressus Internationalis Superiorissarum Generalium*, 1952, p. 277.)

impressed either by the rugged solidarity of institutions or by the antiquity of certain traditions.

In order that authority and obedience may be always founded on genuine spirituality, the patina accumulated by habit must be removed. Thus superiors will never be too sure of their power, and subjects will not be too passive, timid, or hesitant in their submission.

I I

Dialogue Between Superiors and Subjects

I therefore, a prisoner for the Lord, beg you to lead a life worthy of the calling to which you have been called, with all lowliness and meekness, with patience, forbearing one another in love, eager to maintain the unity of the Spirit in the bond of peace. There is one body and one Spirit . . . one Lord . . . one God and Father of us all, who is above all and through all and in all.

Eph. 4:1-6

FOR A long time most Congregations gave little thought to the formation of superiors, as if nomination or election conferred the needed competence. If some qualities were lacking, it was hoped superiors would acquire them in the process of forming their subordinates. Besides, did they not have the 'grace of state'? Thus consciences were appeased and incompetence tolerated under cover of this convenient and pious alibi.[1]

But in recent years the trend has changed. Not only have large Congregations implemented formation sessions for their superiors, but the Union of Major Superiors has called the attention of its members to the need of forming local

---

[1] It is certain that superiors receive from the Holy Spirit graces needed for the exercise of their office. But it is false to say that these graces dispense them from possessing the human qualities and supernatural virtues necessary for this office, and that they replace them. The contrary view is too often held.

185

superiors, and all concerned are making a study of this vital problem. The present chapter, compiled with the help of various documents,[1] constitutes a rapid sketch of the problem in question, with some of its solutions.

I. FUTURE SUPERIORS MUST BE SELECTED

It is important to discern early in young religious the basic qualities necessary for governing.

Qualities of the mind—prudence and good judgement, ability to distinguish essentials from details; a sense of discretion and moderation. Intuitive psychological insight should be developed within an appropriate culture.

Qualities of the heart—kindness, goodness, and capacity to love in the most supernatural sense, springing from self-denial and total self-forgetfulness, and manifesting themselves in a willingness to give up time, talents and heart to all, even the most troublesome, without seeking any return, in constant charity.

Qualities of the will—characteristics of leadership, a spirit of initiative and decision, or organization and of firmness tempered with kindness.

These qualities should be developed by the exercise of controlled but gradually increasing responsibilities, through practice in handling persons and situations.

Supernatural dispositions—a solid interior life, union with our Lord preparing the soul for that 'solitude with God' which is often the lot of a superior; humility and thanksgiving in the spirit of the Magnificat, very firm theological virtues, unshakable fidelity to the Church and to her Congregation, apostolic zeal.

Well-balanced health is also important. . . .

Who should not be chosen:

[1] *Bulletin de l'Union des Supérieures Majeures*, Nov. 1958; *Directoire des Supérieures*, series. 'Problèmes de la Religieuse d'Aujourd-'hui;' the community bulletins of several Congregations, graciously loaned by the superiors general of these Congregations.

Religious who are too young, lacking in maturity and experience at the spiritual and religious level, as well as at the human level; those who do not have sufficient health to maintain the effort required by the office; those in whom one faculty predominates at the expense of the others and of good general balance: who are either too intellectual, or too impressionable, or too authoritarian, etc.[1]

Not all these qualities are needed at once in their perfection; time is given by God to all, even superiors, for progress in the virtues of their state. However, one or other quality must not be radically lacking.

Nor should greater importance be given to any one group of qualities—those of the supernatural or apostolic life, or those pertaining to human equilibrium. They are all equally important because they are irreplaceable.

Nevertheless, the importance of the so-called natural virtues should not be overlooked:

Sincerity. If a superior is sincere, her subjects will be sincere, and there can be no human or supernatural education without an atmosphere of sincerity and honesty.

Tact, which will permit fraternal charity to express itself in actions and foresight indicative of love.

Discretion, which encourages confidence in that it gives sisters the assurance that what they tell their superior will never be confided to others, nor be one day used against them.

Calmness and peace. A peaceful superior spreads peace around her. Such a climate is indispensable for the full maturation of persons within obedience. The superior should not take a tragic view of small matters; let her have a sense of humour and be able to laugh.

[1] *Bulletin de l'Union des Supérieures Majeures*, Nov. 1958.

II. THEY MUST BE TAUGHT THE ART OF COMMUNICATION

Dialogue is more than an art, it has become a science; and those destined to enter into personal relationships with others have much to learn from case-work methods. However, the purpose of these pages is not to describe the technique of dialogue, but rather to explain its necessity.

We have seen that the superior is called to be the educator of her sisters. This is her essential function. Since her role will be to promote their human, spiritual and apostolic development, she must first realize this development within herself. Thus she will be able to foster in others a similar maturity, defined as the full flowering of the love of God and of the neighbour, including love of self. Having learned to recognize the obstacles to her own maturity, she will be able to lead others to recognize such manifestations in themselves. If, for example, their affectivity is underdeveloped, she will encourage them to open their hearts to others and forget themselves, making them able to love by giving them the occasion to do so.

It has been said that the lay apostolate in the modern world constitutes an obstacle to religious obedience. This explanation is frequently given for the scarcity of religious vocations. Such opinions are unquestionably false. How can the lay apostolate, willed and prescribed by the Church, lead to a lack of esteem for the religious state through contempt for obedience? What does happen, however, is that the formation of a lay apostle makes it very difficult for her to accept passive obedience not founded on dialogue with authority.

It is true that the modern girl has become accustomed to discuss problems with others and to take part in consultations, but only in order to seek and find the will of God and the teaching of the Lord in a particular case. Catholic Action properly understood is a school of obedience founded on a continual dialogue with God, with the Church, and with others. When a person so formed enters religion, she expects to find God's will in the same way, by similar discussion with her superior. No doubt the latter's authority will be firmer than that of a Catholic Action team because it bears a different character; but submission to the judgement of another in teamwork is excellent training in obedience to God and the superior who represents him.

In a dialogue between the superior and the sister, who is to take the initiative? Normally it is the superior, at least if she is mature. But sometimes, when time is not ripe, she may have to wait discreetly. She must leave nothing undone to make it easy for the religious eventually to approach her, and when she does, let her listen with patience, without within thirty seconds appealing to the 'motive of faith'.

The dialogue must take place in humility and peace of heart. Each must trust the other sufficiently to believe that she is seeking what God wants. This is why both must previously have consulted God in prayer, and must remain alert to his will during the conversation, which in this way will take place at the proper level and normally result in obedience. But if each has made up her mind and determined her point of view in advance without reference to the divine will, if she has her mind set on getting what she wants at any cost, then there will result only a conflict of two human wills. A mutual search for the will of God, on the other hand, becomes for both a means of spiritual growth; the sister can go as far as the second-last word, while the superior has the last. The rights of authority are fully safeguarded and the duties of the subject truly fulfilled; but the personal growth of both is likewise assured.

The following is a description, by a professional woman psychologist, of the sentiments which should animate a superior at the time of the interview.

Suppose a sister arrives in your office. Forget for the time being all that you know about her, in order that it may not prove an obstacle. . . . Give your intuitive sense full play, for it will enable you better to understand the sister you do not know. . . .

Smile at her. Listen to her completely, with all your heart; give your whole attention to her, not to what you are about to say.

This will not prevent your remaining master of the situation.

Welcome her emotion, her suffering. Look at her intently, beyond the mask of her face.

Try to sense what she cannot say because she is not aware of it; what she feels, what lies behind her words. Above all, do not impose your ideas on her.

Preserve this attitude if you want to help her for her own sake, and not merely to exercise your influence over her.

Put her at her ease by asking her in a calm, friendly way what she would like to say, then listen to her in silence, with a word of encouragement now and then. Do nothing else than listen.

If you are in a hurry and have only a few minutes to spare, you must be even more calm, more silent, as if this were all you had to do all day. This is the time to live the present moment and forget all the rest. . . .

Listen objectively to what she has to say, putting yourself in her place and bearing in mind that even if she is at fault, you have no right to judge her, still less to condemn her. Sense the difference there is between condemning a person, and explaining to her kindly and affectionately that she has wandered from what she should have done and that reparation is necessary, that you are obliged to be severe, not in order to punish her, but to protect her from herself. Acts must always be considered apart from individuals; the act and not the person must be judged. As for the latter, always give her credit for good will and good intentions.

Listen from the heart. This soul needs your faith in her, her potentialities and her desire to do better. She needs your respect for her sorrow, her suffering, her failings, herself. She needs your encouragement to help her advance. She needs to feel that you are taking her seriously, that you are ready to entrust her with some responsibility, and that her progress really means something to you.

It is by trusting everyone and believing in their power for good that you will achieve results undreamed-of. Your faith in others will enable them to have faith in you and in themselves. . . .

What they expect from you is a little genuine love which will help them bear their difficulties, and give them the hope that they have not failed, but can repair and build. . . .

We are not always aware of the effect we have on others. Perhaps we are hurting them without knowing or meaning it. Curiosity and indiscreet questions cause harm by obliging others to speak when they do not wish to, and then they withdraw into themselves. In certain cases it is necessary to refuse to listen to confidences and consider the present only, for only present fulfilment matters. The past should be referred to only in so far as it casts light on the present. Otherwise it is unprofitable rumination. Do not abruptly cast aside an unpremeditated thought. Give the reasons why it would not be useful. . . .

You will then understand that a sister is bestowing a wonderful gift on you by providing you with an occasion of giving her something. It is you who owe her thanks and esteem.

Watch her leave with your heart full of gratitude in that she has done more for you than you for her—she has provided you with an occasion of giving yourself to others.

III. SUPERIORS MUST BE TAUGHT TO PROMOTE INITIATIVE WITHIN OBEDIENCE

A superior must be able to delegate her authority and give orders that leave room for true initiative. That type of authority which controls every detail and manifests a sort of mental myopia alienates subjects. An adult superior wants about her subjects who are also adults. She will not be afraid to let them take the initiative, and will accept the risks involved. In case of failure, she does not crush the individual. Just as God does not want slaves at his service, so the superior wants religious who are able to stand on their own feet, and she will foster this by allowing them to assume responsibility. When a superior trusts her subordinates she gains their confidence, just as her honesty wins theirs.

True, it is always a risk not to foresee and regulate every detail; but the acceptance of such a risk will involve wholesome self-denial on the part of the superior. Nothing is more efficacious for the formation of a religious and for her sound human development than the gift of a responsibility suited to her capacities. One major superior writes: 'A person who is not made to reflect, choose, and carry real responsibility towards others will act mechanically and gradually be impoverished.' It is understood that the temperament, capability, experience and limitations of each one must be taken into account.

In entrusting responsibility to a religious, the superior must be able to ask three things of her: that she accept it wholly and courageously; that she carry it out with all her heart and strength; that she be ready at any moment to submit it to the control of the superior. This being understood, the superior should be very broad in her control and reserved in giving advice which might have the force of commands.

This attitude of superiors can be of great value in the apostolate. It is an enormous waste of time for religious to have to refer every slightest detail to the superior. But when the superior has faith in the good will and competence of her sisters, she is providing dynamic leadership from within, and she reveals to her subjects themselves, aptitudes and powers which they never suspected they possessed.

Such is the attitude of the Church towards Christians. She allows them the freedom to go wherever the Holy Spirit leads them; sometimes she closes off certain dangerous or inopportune ways, but she does not impose upon them a uniform or prefabricated orientation. Père de Montcheuil writes:

> To be able to walk without awaiting a push from those in authority, to stop when they indicate a tentative pause, to turn back without hesitation when they issue warning of a wrong path, to have the courage to begin again in ways left open, without ill-humour or discouragement— all these are dispositions which should be familiar to a Catholic. While they may complicate somewhat the discernment of his vocation and his fidelity to God's call, they cannot be said to favour passivity or sloth. By obliging him to give up certain over-simplified attitudes of inertia or revolt, they demand an alertness and an equilibrium which promote growth.[1]

The following advice was compiled by two religious priests engaged in the work of education, for the use of the parents of their students. What is applicable to a mother and father towards their children, is surely so likewise to a superior with regard to her sisters:

> Allow the child to take the initiative in whatever he can reasonably do by himself. . . .

[1] Yves de Montcheuil, *Problèmes de Vie Spirituelle*, pp. 84-5.

Let him assume the responsibility for his actions, and whenever possible, let him take the consequences. . . .

Do not be afraid to trust him with certain responsibilities in the home. . . .

Encourage and accustom the child to make his own way in the outside world, to make contacts with strangers . . . not to be afraid of undertaking things on his own. . . . How many children (and adults) refuse to act, to take the initiative, to express themselves, to react personally in society through fear of the unfamiliar, of the opinions of others, of being conspicuous, through excessive timidity or self-love! Whence that unfortunate sheep-like mentality, that capitulation of the human personality in group life. . . .

Have personal conversations alone with your child. . . . In this way his personality will bud forth. . . . It is easy to pick out in a group those children whose parents treat them as personal friends. . . . These children have more self-assurance and self-confidence. . . .

Let the relationship of children with their parents in the family circle assume the characteristics of a friendly association for the common good. . . . This implies that the child is considered as a young person capable of being serious. . . . Moreover, such an association will require a climate of peace and mutual confidence. . . . These responsibilities must not be given the child as an added burden, but as a positive means of growth and of realizing a work that will give joy to others.[1]

What has been so well said for parents applies perfectly to religious superiors.

[1] P. P. Michel Froidure and Xavier Lefebvre, S.J., *Counsels to the Parents of the Students*, St Joseph's School, Lille.

IV. SUPERIORS MUST LEARN THE ART OF GIVING ORDERS

The name 'superior' is rather misleading in spite of its traditional use in constitutions and in Canon Law. As a result of the vague uneasiness caused by the implications of the word, some effort has been made to invent a more modern one.

The ancient word 'prioress' was more appropriate. A prioress is merely the first in a community, not one who stands on a pedestal from which to issue orders and hurl invectives. So the sister in charge of a community is the first to walk in the way, like the Good Shepherd whom the sheep follow. She is aware of her solidarity with the other religious and tries to give them the example, so that they may walk in her footsteps. If she is simply the first of the sisters she will not impose her power, nor is she likely to speak of her authority. She may, if necessary, speak of the responsibility God has given her and of the will of the Father which she tries, with her sisters, to discover and accomplish.

Nevertheless, the superior has to govern her community. She will have to be firm with certain religious in order to guide them to God. According to the constitutions, she must also direct an institution or works of charity in obedience to the commands she has received from her superior general and according to the directives of the bishop for the co-ordination of the apostolate in his diocese. In this immense field of labour she can do much by example, by counselling, advising, and encouraging. But there still remains an area in which she must issue orders and prohibitions.

In order to do so, she must learn *to foresee*. A command must first be carefully pondered by the one who gives it, examined in the context of the whole situation, compared with the sought will of God, in agreement with the constitutions, the known will of major superiors and the apostolic intentions of the bishop, and finally adapted to the mentality of her who is to receive it. A command should never be improvised for then it risks being mistaken and especially being given in an unpleasant tone.

After being duly prepared and foreseen, it must be given clearly and precisely, and yet with respect for the one who is to carry it out. And, finally, its execution must be supervised; but while the superior should give moderate aid to the recipient, the latter should bear the full responsibility for her actions.

The problem of following up the execution of an order is always a delicate one. The superior must *see for herself* and *be silent* for some time. This includes not only silence of the tongue, but of the eyes and the expression (not to appear annoyed), and of the whole bearing (not to show coldness of manner). She should never transmit to the sister in question reports that have been made by others concerning her. It is well to give her opportunities for speaking so that if she is guilty, she may accuse herself.

Since a superior is responsible for the advancement of her sisters, she must learn the most difficult of arts, that of correcting. She must never humiliate them. Humiliations are rarely the path to humility, still less to love.

Severe reproaches and especially scoldings maintain subordinates not in obedience, but in servility. Such pedagogical methods may on rare occasions be good for children, but even with adolescents a good educator will avoid them. With much greater reason should they be avoided with adults. Even within obedience, when correction must be given, any dialogue between the superior and the sister must always be a dialogue between adults.

An *action* must never be blamed; a good educator takes

the time to investigate the cause. A correction aimed at a faulty act merely scratches the surface and humiliates without educating. The cause may be very deep and very obscure.

Let superiors especially avoid exerting pressure on the conscience of the sisters by such warnings as these: 'I wonder how you can receive Communion in such dispositions.' 'I wonder how God is judging you at this moment.' The conscience of a religious is a delicate one, and so it should be. It must not be infantilized by being transformed into a scrupulous conscience.

Once a deserved correction has been given and even legitimate sanctions imposed, it is important to turn the page and give the sister the certainty that the fault has been forgotten, and that neither in the mind of the superior nor in the files of the Congregation will the slightest judicial record remain of it. She must be allowed to start over again without any handicap. Once more, if she knows that her superior has faith in her, this will be the greatest encouragement she could receive. Is this not how God acts towards us? In spite of our sins he always loves us, and his fatherly indulgence manifests always the same resilience.

The art of giving orders includes also the manner of giving permissions. Certain immature religious go to their superior for the slightest permission and dispense themselves from all reflection. It sometimes happens that superiors fall into the trap, especially if their own meticulous authoritarianism springs from the same immaturity. Obedience must not be allowed to degenerate into a sort of psychological necessity for the infantile, the intellectually lazy, or those inclined to routine. The fact of asking or obtaining a permission does not dispense a religious from her responsibility before God. Obedience is not an easy way of quieting the conscience.

When a religious asks a permission, she must have already passed judgement on the matter before God. Then only should she approach her superior to have this judgement ratified or otherwise. An adult religious engages herself in the way of obedience with faith and love in order to protect herself against her weakness and her impulsiveness. She seeks to unite herself to the calls of the Holy Spirit which she hears within, and submits them to the judgement of her superior. Within the most complete submission, she is the one responsible and she knows it. It belongs to the superior to command in such a way that the religious will never lose the sense of her responsibility in God's sight. When she comes for a permission, it would be well for her superior sometimes to ask her what she herself thinks of it before God.

This being understood, the superior must not answer as though granting an authorization were an evil. She will either grant it or not. If the answer is yes, let it not be given reluctantly; if it is no, let the sister see that she minds refusing.

It will sometimes happen that the superior is mistaken. This is not a catastrophe; no one is infallible in the exercise of authority. Even the most carefully weighed commands may be erroneous. The worst thing to do in such a case is to persist in the error and try to justify it. There is something noble about a superior's recognizing her mistake. She thus strengthens her authority by taking it down from its false human pedestal, and elevates the sister's obedience to the level of faith.

It is indeed very difficult to be a superior, and it is an art one has never finished learning. Humanly speaking, a superior is very much alone. No doubt she can and must count on the advice and support of higher superiors. But within the community itself of which she is only the first religious, she must accept a true solitude. It is already much to know and accept the fact from the start; but gradually, as time wears on, the superior must be strong enough to bear her anxieties alone and resist the instinctive need of seeking a confidant. This confidant would soon become a favourite, causing ill-will and jealousy in the community. If, however, she wishes to share her concerns with all the religious, let it be done rather as a manifestation of the trust she places in them, than as a means of unburdening her mind. It has been said with reason that the first supernatural disposition required in a future superior is the capacity to endure the 'solitude with God' which will be her lot.

It is true that she who has chosen the Lord is alone only when she forgets him. Solitude with God means isolation only in a human sense. This is indeed an austere life, but a life truly full. A heart that loves does not suffer from solitude.

Finally, the superior will derive strength from the sacrament of penance. But she must remember that the perfection of her state cannot be acquired by mere efforts of the human will. It will above all be the result of humble daily prayer nourished by the conviction of her profound wretchedness and the joy of co-operating in the work of the Lord, Shepherd and Servant.

IV

Hard Work and Evangelization?

The world will belong to him who loves it most and proves it best.

Curé d'Ars

What I find striking in Jesus is his urge always to go forward; so that it might be said that the stable element in Christianity consists in never standing still.

Henri Bergson

THE FIRST part of this work surveyed briefly the decreasing number of religious, the difficulty of recruitment, the increasing average age of the sisters, and the suppression of many well-established missions. But there are still many religious on active duty, as well as an adequate number of priests, in most urban centres of the western world.

Yet when sisters, actively engaged in the apostolic activities in which they spend themselves so unsparingly today, pause a moment to survey the results of their labours, certain disturbing facts emerge which cause no small concern to those who are willing to look beyond the reassuring zone of statistics to the actual reality.

The dechristianization of the world at large goes on apace. The majority of those who have come under the direct influence of religious do not appear noticeably different from others. They do not seem able to resist the corrosive influence of the world; the solid personal spiritual life and vigorous Catholic leadership one would expect to find among the graduates of our Catholic schools and colleges, seem strangely lacking.

Religious are not alone to blame; but since we are here concerned with a study of the religious sisterhoods in the twentieth century, I shall limit myself to a consideration of these only, and of the conditions which would promote their greater apostolic fruitfulness.

Their devotion to duty is unquestionable. No one is more devoted than a religious, and religious have never been more devoted than they are today; or at least they have never worked so hard.

Let no one mistake my meaning. The value of devotion to duty must not be minimized on the plea that it does not yield tangible results. The conversion of souls operates at a level that escapes consciousness and into which one can enter only by faith. It is obtained especially by the paradoxical means, 'prayer and fasting'—humble means. This is why devotion to duty, when inspired by charity and lived in faith, possesses a power to convert which cannot be measured in numbers.

But what kind of devotedness are we speaking of? Its motivation is complex and its driving power is psychological as well as spiritual. It depends on temperament as well as faith, and we are always in danger of baptizing 'zeal for souls' what is only a more or less disordered expression of uncontrolled need for activity. It is possible to be very generous, and never show forth the person of Christ. It is possible to be devoted to duty and show forth nothing but oneself.

However, this is not the point. There is much greater need of spreading the Gospel message than of working hard, and a world of difference exists between the two. What is required of modern apostles is that they evangelize the world. Their work has apostolic value only in so far as it leads souls to amend their lives, in so far as it is a 'word', that is, a revelation of the Word Incarnate. They are expected to announce the person of the Lord and the saving message that he has brought, in order to engage men in a way of fundamental conversion.

I shall first explain the meaning of evangelization. Then we shall be able to discern a few causes of our failure to evangelize the world in spite of the powerful means used and the energy spent. This will enable me to suggest a few remedies designed to restore to the work of religious the evangelizing power that it should exert according to the plan of God.[1]

This treatment of the subject, as well as the rest of this work, is obviously not intended to be exhaustive. We can only contribute to the profound effort of reflection going on in the Church, and at the same time render homage and support to those Congregations which in the course of the past few years have had the courage completely to renew their methods in the work of the apostolate.

[1] Cf. Rev. E. Gambari of the S. Cong. of Rel., on the mandate of active religious in the Church.

12

Communicating the Good News

Brethren . . . to us has been sent the message of this salvation.

Acts 13:26

Go into the whole world and preach the Gospel to every creature.

Mark 16:15

THE WORD 'evangelization', though as old as the Gospel itself, is being used increasingly today. In the past, priests, catechists, and religious believed that it was sufficient to teach, and the faith would flourish spontaneously in a Christian society. The problem simply resolved itself by means of instruction in Christian doctrine. Nothing could be more false and more illusory.[1]

When later the citadel of Christianity was threatened on every side, the science of apologetics was added to doctrine. Although apologetics are useful in strengthening the faith of a believer and showing that it is not contrary to reason, very few unbelievers have been converted by it. More should not be demanded of this science than it is able to give.

Evangelization, then, does not consist merely in expounding or defending Christian doctrine. Nor does it consist in

[1] Cf. Abbé R. Girault, *Pour un catholicisme évangélique*, Economie et Humanisme, Editions Ouvrières, 1959.

'saving souls'. The expression is inaccurate. The soul is separated from the body only by death, and this is a violent, un-
natural state which will definitively come to an end at the
resurrection. It is sometimes said that the soul was created
in the image of God; this is false, for according to the Bible,
this divine likeness resides in *man*.[1] Christ came to bring
salvation to man, that is, the salvation of the body as well as
that of the soul.[2]

Evangelization does not consist in 'implanting the
Church', that is, creating institutions in the hope that the
faith will thus be propagated. Institutions do not precede
faith; on the contrary, community of faith must precede the
erection of churches and schools, and the modern tragedy is
that very often the latter have preceded the former and
prevented its progress.

To evangelize a person is to lead him to a sufficient knowledge of Jesus Christ the Saviour, so that henceforth, in virtue of the laws of supernatural growth under the influence
of the gifts of the Holy Spirit, he may arrive at a knowledge
of the total mystery revealed in Jesus Christ, and surrender
his whole life to this mystery. 'Every one who calls upon the
name of the Lord will be saved. But how are men to call upon
him in whom they have not believed? And how are they to
believe in him of whom they have never heard? And how
are they to hear without a preacher? . . . So faith comes
from what is heard, and what is heard comes by the preach-

---

[1] Moreover, the Bible tells us that it is in man and woman as one
that the likeness of God is to be found. Other currently used expressions should likewise be re-examined. Prayer is not an elevation of
the soul to God, but an elevation of the whole human person, body
and soul together. Personal purification does not require detachment from the body, i.e., from what is sensible, but rather detachment from the original sin of egoism. Cf. *supra*, Part I, Chapter 3.

[2] This proved a scandal to the Greeks (Acts 17: 32).

ing of Christ' (Rom. 10:13-17). 'No one can say "Jesus is the Lord!" except by the Holy Spirit' (I Cor. 12:3).

The purpose of this chapter is to show that evangelization involves three closely interdependent stages.

I. Teaching men the Christian mystery in its totality

II. Revealing the total Christian mystery to men through the witness given by the apostle's entire life

III. Men's gradual discovery of the totality of the Christian mystery in their own lives

These three steps must obviously be identified and studied separately, but *there must always be present to our mind the necessity of uniting them closely*, otherwise there can be no evangelization. The latter cannot be partial or incomplete. Either it is accomplished or it is not. This evangelization will, it is true, be progressive, for the education given by the Holy Spirit is a genuine formation, and he takes all the time necessary to make it succeed. But such a progressive education implies that the entire teaching is implanted as a seed at the beginning. When the apostle awakens in someone the primary realization that Jesus is the Lord and Saviour, this elementary act of faith in the neophyte contains in germ his adhesion to the totality of the mystery, the perceiving of this mystery through the witness to it given by the apostle in his life and the ability to recognize its realization in his own.

I. TEACHING MEN THE CHRISTIAN MYSTERY IN ITS TOTALITY

Christianity is not primarily a moral code with multiple prescriptions, nor a collection of religious practices, nor even a series of dogmas studied and taught separately.

It is a mystery which is totally accepted in the first act of faith, in the first conversion and the first surrender, within which new riches are unceasingly discovered. It can be compared to a cathedral seen for the first time, whose ever new wonders need a lifetime to admire. Or again, it is like a many-faceted diamond, each facet contributing its own particular lustre which is itself a reflection of the whole.

I shall endeavour to describe some of these facets and wonders; but we must remember that not one of them is first among the others, and that each one exists within the whole and reflects a part of the beauty of the whole.

1. *Christianity is Good News*, a message of joy, a certainty of deliverance brought to captives condemned to death, on the morning of their execution.

The angel of the Annunciation says to Mary, 'Rejoice.'[1] Mary's spirit 'rejoices' in God her Saviour (Luke 1:46). The angel says to the shepherds, 'Behold, I bring you good news of a great joy which will come to all the people' (Luke 2:10). In his very first preaching at Nazareth, Jesus proclaims that he has come to fulfil the prophecy of Isaiah: 'The Spirit of the Lord is upon me, because he has anointed me to preach good news to the poor. He has sent me to proclaim release to the captives . . .' (Luke 4:18; Is. 61:1-2). And after the last supper he bestows the gift of his joy on his disciples (John 15:11; 16:22; 16:24), and he prays the Father to grant it to them (John 17:13).

If the Gospel is Good News in the original and etymological sense of the word, each of its pages is Good News as well. To spread the Gospel is to spread joy, a joy so dynamic and irrepressible that it cannot be contained within, but must at any cost be shared. Yet in the eyes of most unbelievers, 'the

---

[1] This is the true meaning of the word 'Ave', a much stronger meaning than the mere 'Hail' (Luke 1:28).

Church appears as an insulated society in the hands of an antiquated hierarchy whose business it is to promulgate interdicts and restrictions and create a world in which people are bored'.[1]

Unbelievers do not know the Church; this is why they harbour such misconceptions. But how are they to know her true physiognomy except by its reflection on our own? Why do we present an aspect so serious and severe? If the generality of Christians were really acquainted with the joy of the resurrection, this joy would inevitably find its way to the exterior.[2] It must be clearly understood, however, that there is no question here of 'appearing' or 'pretending'; we cannot appear exteriorly to be what in fact we are not within. Besides, this is not a selfish or a sentimental joy, still less a physiological joy. It is the joy of the salvation of the world in Christ.

Evangelization can assume forms as varied as the activities in the life of an apostle, but the message transcends all these activities. It embodies all deeds and gives them such dynamism, such significance and such value, that all who see the apostle at work can discover through his activity the 'Good News' he longs to transmit.

Religious are everywhere the vanguard of the Church. They assume the most varied forms of the charity of the Church and the most heroic. Yet they will be authentic witnesses to this charity only if, in and through all their activity, they can communicate the wondrous discovery they themselves have never finished making, and which they renew daily. Their most self-sacrificing activity will bear no

---

[1] Girault, *op. cit.*, p. 44.

[2] *Ibid.* Bernanos writes: 'You may be in the state of grace, but after all, it isn't very evident. What have you done with the grace of God? Shouldn't it radiate from you? Where the deuce do you hide your joy?' (*Les grands cimetières sous la lune*, p. 253.)

evangelical fruit if they are not penetrated with a joy ever new and ever renewed at the living source.[1]

2. *This Good News is that God is alive, and we know it from the living Christ.*

God is 'someone'—this was what Claudel discovered with wonderment on the day of his conversion. The Gospel, for one who reads it with Christ, is a revelation of the Father. Jesus is always with his Father; his name is always on his lips because his heart is full of him. He 'praises' or 'blesses' him unceasingly; he 'seeks' his will, and his 'food' is to accomplish that will. He discerns his Father in all the signs of his presence: the birds he feeds, the flowers he clothes, the face of a child reflecting his face. Christ did not leave to his apostles a treatise on the Trinity; but he revealed the Father to them by living with him in their sight, showing them by daily experience what it means to walk in the presence of the 'living God' (I Kings 17:1).

The apostles who knew Jesus do not speak of him as one who existed in the past, but one who is now alive. Read the first verses of the first Epistle of St John (I John 1:1-4), or the first Epistle of St Peter: 'Without having seen him you love him; though you do not now see him you believe in him and rejoice with unutterable and exalted joy. As the outcome of your faith you obtain the salvation of your souls' (I Peter 1:8-9). All the Epistles of St Paul especially are vibrant with the continual and actual presence of the life of Jesus in him.

For Saint Paul, nothing matters any longer but Christ. Not human fulfilment . . . but the Mystery of the Crucified. 'I decided to know nothing among you except Jesus

[1] 'Behold, God is my salvation; . . . for the Lord God is my strength and my song, and he has become my salvation. With joy you will draw water from the wells of salvation' (Is. 12:2-3).

Christ and him crucified.' The world? 'The world has been crucified to me, and I to the world.' Will he hold on to some apparently valuable assets, through respect for human values? 'For his sake I have suffered the loss of all things, and count them as refuse, in order that I may gain Christ.' To live with Christ, and for Christ to live in him —this is all he is interested in. He has other things to do than to seek the development of his human personality. And when he considers the history of man, at the centre of his vision are the tragedy of sin and the bloody Sacrifice of Calvary. This contemplative who has seen Jesus and heard ineffable words which man is not permitted to reveal, cannot escape this 'obsession' of God.

He has only one desire: 'To depart and be with Christ'. . . . And what does he teach the faithful? 'If you have been raised with Christ, seek the things that are above where Christ is, seated at the right hand of God. Set your minds on things that are above, not on things that are on earth. . . . Your life is hid with Christ in God.' 'We look not to the things that are seen but to the things that are unseen; for the things that are seen are transient, but the things that are unseen are eternal.' He does not confuse charity with every kind of service to others: 'If I give away all I have, and if I deliver my body to be burned, but have not love, I gain nothing. . . .' All things will pass away—learning, service, the apostolate; discoursing, theology, speculation will have an end. Alone, charity in contemplation before God will endure: then we shall see him face to face.[1]

So must it be with every apostle. It is not enough for him to be convinced of the existence of Jesus Christ. At the very moment when he is speaking or acting, he must 'see' the living Christ unceasingly revealing his Father. If men do not see us living in the presence of God with all possible vitality,

[1] R. Père Paissac, 'Le sens de Dieu', *La Vie Spirituelle*, July 1946, pp. 22-3.

the message will not get through. Perhaps they will say, 'He speaks well.' 'He is dedicated to his work.' But they will think, 'He is only doing what he must', and they will not see the Lord.

3. *This Good News is that God is love*, that he cannot but love, and that his very nature is to be love (I John 4:8; 4:9-13). The most overwhelming revelation is that God Almighty is love itself, that this love has prompted him to send us his only Son, and that the latter, *by his life, death, and resurrection*, has borne witness to the love of the Father.

To say that God is love and that Jesus is the Saviour is not enough. The love of God for us was proved when he gave us his only Son (John 3:16). Jesus is the Saviour, not only from the day he received his name (Matt. 1:18), but when he gave his life for us; there is 'no greater love' than this (John 15:13). The Christian message must go thus far; it must dare to preach the scandal of the cross of Jesus. It is true that Christ is risen and we must never forget to announce it; but he rose only because he had first died. The most urgent message Christ had to give to the disciples of Emmaus on Easter day was that of the indissoluble link between his death and his resurrection, and the absolute necessity of passing through suffering to enter into glory (Luke 24:26).

He who discovers the personal love of God for him in giving him his only Son, and the personal love of Jesus for him in giving him his life, cannot keep such a discovery to himself. He will learn by experience that such love is poured forth upon him only to be lavished by him on all his brothers.

4. *The Good News is communicated by the Church and within the Church.*

Christ is inseparable from the Church which he founded and in which he lives mysteriously. The future Christian will be able to find Christ either by meeting a person who seriously lives his faith, or within a Christian community in the midst of which he lives. But it is always to the Church he is led, like Saint Paul who, after the miracle on the road to Damascus, went to the Church in the person of Ananias (Acts 9 : 10-29). In the words of Cardinal Feltin, 'Evangelization consists in revealing Jesus Christ living in the Church, in and by means of an encounter with others.'[1] The Church is more than a milieu within which Christ is given; she is a person, the bride of Christ (Eph. 5 : 25; Apoc. 21) who leads men to him.

When a new Christian begins to discover the true nature of the Church, he senses that he has become a member of an immense family, and daily comes in contact with very dear brothers, for whom he knows he is responsible. It is within the Church that brotherly love can flourish, upheld by the desire for family growth and family expansion without limit.

5. *The Good News possesses a dynamism such that he who receives it must one day be converted and become a new man.*

As long as the message has not changed the heart of him to whom it is addressed, there is no evangelization. The Good News of salvation through Christ cannot be received passively. The mercy of God is such that we are called to take an active part and be true collaborators in this salvation. To become a new man is to consent to change one's life and adopt an entirely new scale of values.

Notwithstanding the opinion of its enemies and even of many Christians, Christianity is not a comfortable way of life. True, it brings peace; but this peace resides beyond the sensibilities (Phil. 4 : 7), and is normally accompanied by a wholesome disquiet. The essential question is this : What is the place of Christ in our concept of existence? Is he only a

[1] Allocution of 20 March, 1957.

part of it, even a very important part? Then we are still very far from him; we are not converted. But if, on the contrary, Jesus Christ is all our life and we refer all things to him, then we begin to be new men. 'Salvation in him is not a sort of *refuge* in the human sense; . . . it is rather a life lived with him and in him, something more like an *adventure* with all its risks.'[1] For this reason a newly converted man can never rest, like a mountain climber who has reached the top. He cannot rest until he has helped all his brothers who are still in the plains to follow the same road. He will, therefore, never cease from his labours until death.

6. *Finally, this Good News continually enlarges the heart by letting in ever more brothers.* Since he has been converted to Christ living in the Church, and has discovered the love of the Father, in the same glance he takes in *all his brothers who are children of the same Father.*

Furthermore, he does not see them as distinct and separate individuals, but as diverse elements of one being, the total Christ, as branches of one vine (John 15), and members of one same body (Rom. 12; I Cor. 12).

Having reached this point in the revelation of the Christian mystery, we become aware that each facet, while seeming to disclose but a part of the whole, leads in reality to the very centre of the mystery. The brothers we discover in love recall to us the Father who loves us to the point of giving us his only Son, the Christ who conceals his face beneath the traits of our brothers, and the Church, mother and educator of the children of God. In order to become able to love our brothers, we must be converted and die to ourselves, thus participating in a very concrete and lowly way in the death and resurrection of Jesus.

In a word, the totality of this mystery which we must

[1] Girault, *op. cit.*, p. 48.

teach in the first stage of evangelization is divided by refraction into lights of various colours, but each one leads to the centre, that is, to the Heart of God.

II. REVEALING TO MEN THE TOTAL CHRISTIAN MYSTERY THROUGH THE WITNESS GIVEN BY THE APOSTLE'S ENTIRE LIFE

To obtain conversion of heart, it is not sufficient merely to teach the Christian mystery. Christianity is not transmitted like a profane science—mathematics, or geography. Neither is it received and learned like a profane science. Intellectual knowledge may suffice for both teacher and learner at the level of human subjects; but with regard to the Christian mystery, if it is to lead to the birth of a new man, it must proceed from an apostle who is himself converted and renewed.

This is why one who merely teaches and is not himself by his whole life a witness to the mystery of which he speaks will never truly evangelize, that is, will never lead his hearers to conversion.

It is absolutely necessary for a priest, a religious, or a lay apostle, to be a witness to the mystery; this is, in fact, a condition *sine qua non* of the fruitfulness of his apostolate.

What is a witness? It is not only one who speaks; it is one who, *by his very life*, attests that his words proceed from the Word Incarnate. It is one who, in his apostolic activity, never separates his words from his own life. If he were forced to choose between speaking and living, he would choose to give the witness of his life, for this witness is the foundation of any effective speaking. 'Either the word or the living witness can transmit the message, for the word cannot be dissociated from the witness, and the most silent witness, if it is authentic, speaks as loudly as words in proclaiming that Jesus Christ is living in the Church.'[1] 'A true witness is he who affirms, in the name of an experience he cannot conceal, the existence of a reality no one else can affirm in his place. . . . None can be a witness, therefore, unless he has first lived an experience. . . . And if he is a true witness, he cannot be silent about his experience.'[2] As St Paul says, 'If I preach the Gospel, that gives me no ground for boasting. For necessity is laid upon me. Woe to me if I do not preach the Gospel!' (I Cor. 9 : 16-17).

There is of course no question of devaluing the Gospel to the mere communication of an experience; it is the transmission of a call, the revelation of the Good News. But he who transmits the call must have heard it himself in his heart; he must already have begun to conform his life to it.

In what will the objective elements of such a witness consist?

1. *In the first place, the apostle himself must be estimable at the human level.*

We have already said that for a baptized Christian, there are no natural virtues; all his virtues have supernatural roots.

However, we might utilize in this connection a convenient and generally accepted terminology. A certain number of virtues could, for a non-baptized person, be termed 'preChristian'; and for one who is baptized, 'human' or 'natural' virtues. Let us enumerate them briefly.

Uprightness 'Let what you say be simply "Yes" or "No"' (Matt. 5 : 37). Those who listen to the apostle must know or at least sense that even in matters of minor importance, his words are the limpid expression of his whole thought.

[1] Girault, *op. cit.*, p. 66.
[2] *Ibid.*, p. 67.

To this uprightness must be joined a *sense of justice.* Priests and religious are always in danger of utilizing the resources of moral theology in its casuistic aspect to cover up slightly dishonest practices. They may even sometimes justify these practices by appealing to the alleged benefit to the institution, the Congregation, or even the Church.

Open-mindedness, enabling the apostle always to make the distinction between essentials and accidentals, that is, to hold fast to essentials, and concede a great deal to accidentals. Openness of mind or broad-mindedness does not imply equal acceptance of every opinion, mingling truth and error in the hope that a momentary acceptance of error may prove a stepping-stone to truth. However, an open mind will accept the fact that error may momentarily be mixed with truth; it will clearly bring out the truth and, for the time being, be silent concerning the error. Above all, an open mind will accept delays in spiritual growth, and will not crush beginners beneath the weight of principles they are not yet able to bear.

Strength of character The apostle must have attained maturity and be able to stand on his own feet. This strength of character is particularly necessary for religious. While they live under the yoke of obedience, they must show that obedience admits of and even encourages perfect liberty of thought in all spheres in which it does not come into play. Nothing is more unfortunate for the apostolate of a religious than a manifestation of childish docility in matters in which everyone knows there is no question of obedience. On the other hand, an example of true religious obedience will have all the greater force if it is given by a person psychologically and affectively mature.

Disinterestedness Evangelization is not a matter of working for the advancement of an institution or a Congregation, or even of the Church. Nor is it a matter of 'doing good' and pursuing a self-interested goal under cover of a supernatural motive. It is a matter of simply loving the Lord and loving one's brother with the same impulse of the heart; all the rest will be given besides.

The charity manifested in so many religious houses with such magnificent generosity will have evangelical value only if it is exercised for its own sake, that is, for God and the neighbour, without any self-interested motives even of a supernatural character.

If I give my hungry brother food, it must be first of all because he is hungry, and the instinctive reaction of one who loves as well as the teaching of the Gospel require it —not in order that he may become a Christian. Besides, this pure act of charity without any ulterior motive will no doubt be the best evangelization; for it is easier to see Christ in one who gives in all simplicity, without any of that imperceptible guile which even the most uneducated can always detect.[1]

2. *The apostle must truly live the life of Christ, and this must be visible exteriorly.*

There is no question here of simulation, or of playing a part, or adopting certain more or less religious attitudes, using these as 'methods' to exert a would-be supernatural influence. It is here especially that disinterestedness must be evident. The whole question may be summed up as follows: the apostle must, first and above all, let the life of Christ permeate his own existence through and through; Christ must so live in him that every word he utters is at once stamped with authenticity and reveals, through the human person, the person of Christ who inspires it. Except for a miracle of

[1] Girault, *op. cit.*, p. 69.

grace, a religious can exert no evangelical influence unless Christ lives in her.

This requires much more than fidelity to the constitutions or to exercises of piety, although such fidelity may be a sign of very great love and the means of attaining it. Here again is encountered the problem of religious formation which has already come up in various contexts. The essence of a religious vocation consists in the gift of oneself to Christ and the first and definitive choice one makes of him, and this is indeed a mystery of grace. But while one must pray intensely in order to receive the full benefit of this grace, it is also necessary, through the whole course of one's religious life, to be educated in the art of living in Christ. If, for the religious, to live is Christ, her whole life will speak, even in the silence of the lowliest tasks.

> The priest or Christian who is most skilful in the art of proselytizing is but a worldly prestidigitator if he does not each day make the lowly effort of tending to sanctity. But the holy soul who is at God's disposal evangelizes by her whole life, even if she is awkward at times; the Spirit inspires in her what she must say and do, when Christ must be proclaimed, and when she must simply contribute her fraternal presence, restraining within her impatience to evangelize.[1]

3. *The apostle must be able to bear the cross of Christ, should he meet with it in the course of his apostolic life.*

We have said that the Christian mystery must be communicated in its totality. It is not easy to do so; there is a great temptation to limit the message and eliminate the death and resurrection of the Lord.

The mystery of the cross must of course be taught, and a

---

[1] Girault, *op. cit.*

glance through the Epistles of St Paul will show that it is so much at the core of his message[1] that it cannot be omitted without making the whole incomprehensible. But the first need of an apostle is to live the mystery in his own flesh, lest he find himself preaching in a desert. We have spoken at length of understanding the cross.[2] This cross is as much a 'scandal' in our day as it was at the time of St Paul. This is why it is as necessary for the modern apostle as it was for St Paul, to bear in his body the marks of the Lord Jesus (Gal. 6:17).

Religious are confronted with their own suffering in their daily life before being faced with the suffering of others, and it often happens that their suffering is acute enough to appear exteriorly. Let them not seek to be understood; let them seek no human consolation—only that which comes to them from Christ on the cross. Above all let them not seek consolation from lay persons. Every time they stoop to confide their troubles to seculars, they risk turning them for ever away from the message of the cross. They had something to give, the greatest and most difficult teaching of all, and they closed the door to it. They who represent the Lord because they have consecrated their life to him, cannot bear witness to their union with Christ crucified except by bearing their suffering with faith and courage and proclaiming by their attitude, their hope in the resurrection.

4. *The apostle must live the mystery of charity.*

Here again an accurate understanding is essential. Devotion to duty does not take care of everything and is not alone sufficient to reveal the total Christian mystery. All the self-sacrifice of religious is not enough to convert souls. This may

---

[1] Rom. 3:24-5; 5:10; 6:1-23; 8:32-4; I Cor. 1:17-25; 2:2; 15:3-4; Eph. 2:1-6; 5:2; Phil. 2:5-11; 3:18, etc.
[2] Cf. *supra*, Part II, Chap. 4.

seem paradoxical at first, yet it is true. They are sometimes deceived by the comments of good people who speak with emotion of the devotedness of the 'good sisters' of the parish. But this emotion is very superficial and hardly ever indicative of the beginnings of conversion. Cardinal Liénart declared, 'The only witness able to convert souls is not that of charity in action, but the witness of the unity that exists among members of a community . . . unity also with all those with whom, professionally and apostolically, you must labour.'[1]

Jesus never said that the hard work of his disciples or their charity towards the poor would be a means of conversion. But he did say very explicitly that the conversion of others would depend on the unity existing among those devoted to the apostolate: *'By this all men will know that you are my disciples, if you have love for one another'* (John 13:35). And a few moments after giving them this golden rule, he prayed the Father to give them the grace to do what he had commanded them. 'That they may all be one; even as thou, Father, art in me, and I in thee, that they also may be in us, *so that the world may believe* that thou hast sent me. . . . I in them and thou in me, that they may become perfectly one, *so that the world may know that thou hast sent me'* (John 17:21, 23).

It is, then, not the devotedness shown by religious to outsiders that will bear witness, but the love uniting the members of a community. It is not the isolated religious but the community that evangelizes. In each community there are religious who never speak because they are occupied in administrative or material duties. Others on the contrary, are in contact with people all day long. The silence of the

[1] Concluding discourse at the regional convention of the orders devoted to nursing and social service, Lille, 24 May, 1959.

first is not sterile, nor is the teaching of the second without effect, provided all are united by a bond of true charity, clearly visible to onlookers.

In conclusion let us repeat that it is dangerous to form the habit of spreading the Gospel message by word alone, without also reflecting it by the witness of our life. We can become so accustomed to excel in the art of speaking as to believe ourselves dispensed from living it.

It is in a region far, far beyond mere words that our hearers will recognize the message, receive it, and be converted. They should be able to recognize and receive the message even if the apostle one day became unable to speak. It is perhaps in the life of apostles such as this that those who cannot read or hear could nevertheless receive the essential part of the message.

III. MEN'S GRADUAL DISCOVERY OF THE TOTALITY OF THE CHRISTIAN MYSTERY IN THEIR OWN LIVES

1. *They must first be taught to pray and discover God in their lives.*

Evangelization involves far more than mere indoctrination. If the Gospel could be taught by the same means as any other science it would be very simple; religious would need only to be excellent catechists with adequate certification. But we know that the Christian mystery is discovered only at the end of a personal journey made under the guidance of the Holy Spirit. Thus it is essential that before all else, people be placed on the road to God by prayer. This does not mean getting them to 'say prayers' and teaching them prayer formulas, which however, must also be done at the proper time. But they must be taught that God their Father is near them, unceasingly bending over them in his love; that Christ

is at the centre of their life and heart, and that he continually
solicits them by his Holy Spirit.

This nearness of God must be taught them so vividly that
they will spontaneously experience a need of speaking and
living with him. Why hesitate to do so? True prayer is extremely simple: speaking to God without restraint, and
without concern about phrasing or propriety; or else listening to God in an interior silence which is quite possible even
in the midst of a noisy crowd and the fatigue of work. I have
already treated the matter at length.[1] If priests and religious
use certain methods in praying, it is only in order to arrive
at the goal: a life of prayer. Every human being is called to
such a life in which contact with God becomes spontaneous
at any moment. Often it is sufficient to tell people this, for
them to discover, full of wonder, its possibility. But in order
to tell them about it, the apostle must believe in it himself;
and to believe in it, he must live it. Each time that a religious
reveals to anyone—child, patient, student, convert or lay
worker—how easy it is to converse with God, she places him
at once on the plane of divine grace which alone is able to
convert hearts and transform lives.

Prayer is not an escape from reality. On the contrary, it is
the means of seeing life as it really is. It is a 'revelation' in
the true sense of the word, which is 'to remove the veil'.
For the events of life are covered with a veil beneath which is
hidden God's plan, that is, his love unceasingly at work. Persons are human faces behind which is hidden the face of
God. We must teach others to 'seek the face of God'[2] beneath
the disguises with which it is covered. God is present in circumstances as well as in people, and in the crowds encountered at each turn of the road. If the religious is accustomed

[1] Cf. *supra*, Part II, Chap. 2.
[2] Ps. 24:6; 27:8; 105:4.

to 'see' God in faith, she will feel an urgent need to share her experience with all those whom she meets in her apostolic work.

As early as possible, then, people must be taught to pray and to see through the eyes of faith. If the apostolate of the priest or the religious does not begin there (and unfortunately it often ends without going that far), the message will be cut short and will never reach into the heart and into daily life.

Perhaps this sharing of an experience of prayer will be done more easily in private than in a group. But in any case, a taste for prayer cannot be imparted by words alone, no matter how pious. It is imparted by the witness of words accompanied and permeated by prayer; for the transmission of such a message is the work of grace. It is in this way that Jesus imparted to his apostles a love for prayer and the habit of seeing the Father in persons and circumstances.

2. *They must be taught to recognize the mystery of Christ crucified in their lives.*

In the Church, religious are those who most frequently come in contact with the sufferings of people. Their work is to alleviate them as much as they can and to offer them up at Mass and in their personal and community prayer. But their work is also gradually to enlarge the inner vision of those who suffer, so that they may eventually realize that they are united with Christ crucified and fill up in their flesh what is wanting to the sufferings of Christ for the Church.

Whereas prayer must be taught at the beginning of a soul's education, the mystery of the cross must frequently be held over until the end. In order to do this, the religious must never become accustomed to seeing people suffer. She must enter into their suffering with all her heart and bear it in all her prayer. Those who suffer, either morally or physically, do expect alleviation from religious, but perhaps they expect understanding and sympathy even more. It is a great mistake not to take the time to listen to them; it is perhaps an even greater mistake to speak too soon of the cross of Christ, inviting them to forget their own. It is only after allowing them to empty out their heart, that a religious will be able in due time gently to impart the message of the Lord, the essence of which consists in sharing in the mystery of his death and resurrection. However, while she must await the opportune moment to speak, she must think of it and prepare herself unceasingly by living within herself this mystery of Christ dying and rising again.

3. Finally, *they must be set on the way by charity.*

Since 'love is of God, and he who loves is born of God and knows God' (I John 4:7), every act of brotherly love is a spark of divine love, a sign of true union with God and a means of knowing God. For this reason, evangelization can be founded upon the least gesture of love which all men, even those farthest from God, willingly perform. These acts of brotherly love are more than stepping-stones to further evangelization; they are a sign that this evangelization has already begun in the secret of souls by the unceasing activity of the Holy Spirit. A religious who can recognize these marks of divine grace will use them as a starting point in encouraging and promoting these gestures of brotherly love.

Because 'he who does what is true comes to the light' (John 3:21), the religious will discern wherein those under her care (children, adults, the sick) could 'do what is true' by placing themselves at the service of their fellow men. When he wished to open to the light the Samaritan woman's heart, Christ asked of her the kindness of a drink of water (John

4:7). To open the eyes of the disciples of Emmaus to the
reality of his resurrection, he let himself be invited to eat
with them (Luke 24:29).

To open the eyes of men to the needs of their brothers and
help them bear one another's burdens; to suggest a service,
not for oneself or one's community, but for their own relatives and those in daily contact with them, especially those
most in need—this is the most efficacious way of preparing
their heart to receive the light of God.

Every gesture of the religious is inspired by the love glow-
ing within her.

To approach a soul is, naturally and supernaturally, a
delicate and complicated matter. It requires tact, sympathy, gentleness, patience, discrimination, above all, that
self-effacement which leaves room for grace to pass
and gives to Christ in us the opportunity of touching
hearts. 'Virtus ex illo exibat—Virtue went out from
him.'

This is the very reverse of the 'propagandist' method
which, acting from without, seeks only to impose an
opinion, to violate intimacy, has nothing in view but the
immediate victory to be won. . . . It is a mission of
supreme theological charity to approach a soul in the hope
of leading it nearer to God, of bringing it a message of life
and joy, of drawing it closer to the sacramental sources of
life; to rouse a hesitant or rebellious will. . . .

In dealing with an unbeliever of today who denies God,
Christ, and even the existence of the soul, we must advance
progressively: a full acceptance of religious practice cannot be asked of him, for he does not yet understand its
meaning. This gradual method in religious teaching is not
only lawful but necessary, and is quite a different thing
from putting off evangelization until social relations and
the framework of society have been 'humanized'. . . .

227

Charity must create an atmosphere and prepare hearts. But this patient charity has nothing to do with a dimming of doctrine; it is tense and watchful, not hopeless or defeatist.[1]

[1] Mgr Suenens, *L'Eglise en état de mission*, pp. 188-191. *The Gospel to Every Creature* (Westminster: Newman, 1957), pp. 148-150.

13
Causes of Failure in the Work of Evangelization

The word of God is not fettered.

2 Tim. 2:9

We HAVE seen that the considerable number of religious at work and the very great devotion to duty which they manifest in every sector of the Church's apostolate has not halted the progress of materialism in the world today.

Religious are not alone, nor indeed primarily responsible. The process of paganization depends on factors too complex to be analysed in a work not devoted to the subject. Today every individual is influenced by the whole world, owing to the ease of communication and international exchanges. If we priests and religious examine our consciences, we find that we ourselves have been affected by the same errors and the same routine. We often say that there are too few priests and religious, and we look no further. Should we ever admit that there are still too many priests and religious for the non-essential tasks entrusted to them and the unreasonable manner in which they are expected to work, we would perhaps be enabled to direct our research into new channels and discover hitherto unsuspected solutions to the problem of evangelization.

Moreover, if the definition of evangelization in the preceding chapter is accepted as accurate, we have only to go back over every part of it to show that it is because we have ignored these essential elements that our apostolate has not been more fruitful.

Having made these reservations, we can now examine certain obstacles to evangelization on the part of religious, those proceeding, namely, from psychological unpreparedness, from an incomplete spiritual doctrine and formation, and from a certain rigidity of institutions, works, and functions.

I. THE BARRIER OF PSYCHOLOGICAL UNPREPAREDNESS

Generally speaking, religious prefer not to work with adults, although there is an urgent need for them to do so. Their apostolate has been stunted because they seem afraid to face the realities of life, and they direct their efforts rather towards those who are easier to reach—children, or the sick.

It is relatively easy to take care of children, not only because, psychologically speaking, a child is less intimidating than an adult, but also because it is easier to delude oneself with a child. A child can be taught *prayers*, thus giving the comforting impression that something is being accomplished. The fact that the child has not at the same time been taught *prayer*, is hardly noticeable. A child can easily be taught a certain behaviour, but this will hardly do for an adult.

I do not intend to minimize the importance of apostolic work with children; but it must be admitted that our attention has been almost exclusively taken up with them, and Cardinal Suenens justly observes that 'we lose much of the benefit of that initial work by leaving to their own guidance the young people who go from us when school is over'.[1]

[1] Cardinal Suenens, *op. cit.*, p. 130.

How many sisters devote themselves to the organization of Catholic Action groups or other apostolic work with adults or adolescents, compared with the large number working with children of all ages? And the sick are in the same category as children because of their state of dependence.

The lay apostolate is organized for the most part without religious,[1] except for groups of children, and occasionally of girls. Cardinal Suenens rightly sees in this situation one reason for the diminution of religious vocations. Today vocations are frequently decided later than formerly, that is, between the ages of twenty-five and thirty, and continued contact with the sisters is sometimes what occasions the decision. 'If a nun uses her influence to inspire girls with an apostolic spirit, her relations with them will safeguard vocations and will be easily kept up. If, on the other hand, nuns do not help to smooth the transition from life in the world to the cloister, few girls will offer themselves spontaneously; and the best of them will devote their lives to works of the lay apostolate which have captured their enthusiasm when they left school.'[2]

Sometimes also a long-standing habit of dealing with children creates in religious a certain dictatorial manner which renders relations with adults more difficult. One chaplain of a Catholic Action group remarked with reference to a sister in charge of a residence: 'All our efforts at evangelization are neutralized by her manner of acting; she treats girls of twenty-five as children. . . .'

Moreover, a rigid community life prevents a religious from associating freely with adults. Is it feared she will lose

[1] Religious are not alone responsible for this state of things. Priests have delayed too long in giving them their confidence, and lay apostles inherit the prejudices of their milieu.

[2] Cardinal Suenens, *op. cit.*, pp. 110-111.

her vocation? Lay workers often manifest a sincere desire of associating more intimately with religious; but they encounter a barrier the more insurmountable in that it comes up on every occasion. They observe the kindness and devotedness of the sisters, but regret the fact that they neither know nor understand them. Their life is too hidden, too separated and impenetrable. If religious do not become more accessible, that communion with others in which souls 'open up' can never be established.

II. THE BARRIER OF AN INCOMPLETE SPIRITUAL DOCTRINE AND FORMATION

I am speaking here of the spiritual teaching given by religious to others, but obviously, this teaching is closely dependent upon the teaching which they themselves received. And they received it not only in the novitiate, but during the years of their childhood and adolescence; they were the heirs to a whole presentation of Christian doctrine given to preceding generations, which has been justly censured. It consisted of catechism composed of abstract formulas, in isolation from biblical and even evangelical sources; a dry moral code separated from dogma, and subjecting Christians twenty centuries after the death and resurrection of Christ, to the tyranny of the law.

True, all this has been changed, and there are few domains in which a renewal of spirit has been more evident than in the teaching of religion. But it is not in twenty years that the results of former training can be counteracted, nor can this be done without many precautions to discern and avoid the dangers of thoughtless reaction.

The apostolate of religious is often rendered fruitless by deformations which will now be rapidly described.

1. *Moralism*

This consists not only in reducing Christianity to the practice of morality, and in divorcing morality from the living roots of dogma, but especially in consenting to live in the shelter of principles without regard to persons. At its worst, moralism sees in the spiritual life only sins to be avoided. It manifests itself concretely in detailed examinations of conscience in which all of life is, as it were, peeled away to find out what sins should be avoided, instead of the love of God and our neighbour and the quest to prove it more and more. A formation founded on such negative principles is falsified from the start. A priest in charge of a catechism class remarked that children taught by the sisters were 'more preoccupied with the avoidance of sin than with the positive aspect of Christianity'.

On such a view the moral law weighs with such force and severity upon consciences that it prevents people from making use of their weaknesses and errors as means of growth. The precepts of Christianity have indeed an absolute value, but only because they are precepts of the Lord and the way to his love. The Epistles of St Paul are full of precepts of morality, but none is ever given without an explicit reference to Christi,[1] and when Christ himself in the Gospel gives rules of life, he never does so without an explicit reference to the will of the heavenly Father.[2]

Christian life is a process of continual growth; it includes the experience of weaknesses and falls on the way, and, by this means, the progressive discovery of the power of the grace of God. But if the Christian life is made to consist only in avoiding sin (or rather sins), there is a danger of forming

[1] For example, Rom. 12; 13; 14; II Cor. 9; Gal. 5; Eph. 5, etc.
[2] For example, Matt. 5 and 6.

233

childish consciences and burying the Good News beneath an accumulation of crushing burdens.

This deformation also finds expression in an exaggeration of the importance of the virtue of chastity which is often given precedence over faith and charity. This is not the result of a particular esteem for virginal consecration, but rather the projection of unavowed complexes. Children and girls submit passively to this teaching given in the form of certain restrictions, attitudes, and behaviour. But they will some day discover that a form of Christianity which makes for self-suppression does not answer their most profound needs, and in ridding themselves of these unwholesome practices, they will also reject the good from which they originated. Some educational establishments still endeavour to 'protect' girls by removing all literature relative to the transmission of life, in the belief that 'they will learn these things soon enough'. I am acquainted with one mistress of novices who refused to answer the legitimate queries of a postulant, saying, 'I do not speak of such things. I am a virgin.'

2. *False supernaturalism*

The attitude adopted during the novitiate has its repercussion in the entire life of the apostle, and consequently on evangelization. Too often religious are still trained to be devout and regular and to neglect none of their 'exercises', but in a composed, rigid, and even unthinking way. Why? Great efforts are made for the perfection of psalmody, which is a good thing; and for the uniformity of movement, which is perhaps less good. In rigidity and monotony in religious ceremonies there is an inherent danger of gradually emptying prayer of its soul and its substance. Apostles are needed for the twentieth century—sisters who live in prayer amid their activity and in a sense because of their activity, so true is it that far from being a danger to prayer, activity should nourish it.[1] There is real danger in thus emphasizing external behaviour and regularity—a danger of losing the spirit of prayer while consciences are at peace because a favourable appearance is presented. It must be repeated again and again —and I am under the impression of not saying it emphatically enough—that the formation of religious is always in danger of being both artificial and superficial, because of the schedule of exercises within which it must be enclosed. If there is not a close link between prayer and the real life of a religious, prayer will be only a veneer applied to the exterior and will not reach into the depths of her being. Does it not sometimes happen that a life of 'piety' co-exists with a grievance and even a quarrel with someone?

The concept of the noviceship as a 'garden enclosed' should be re-examined, for it leads to a 'self-centred individualism'.[2] So much emphasis is placed on personal sanctification that postulants form the habit of living a sort of dual existence. Cardinal Suenens writes:

> Even the holiest things may be wrongly used. The care for personal perfection, ill grasped, may lead to a lessening of generosity. Often, before entering the college or novitiate, young people have known the ardour of apostolic generosity in some Catholic Action group. They have been led to enter religious life by the desire of giving themselves wholly to the apostolate. This desire, if deprived through six years or more of all nourishment, may wither away. It is hoped that the sacred fire, kept smouldering under the embers, will blaze up again when exposed to the open air at the end of the period of training. This expectation may be ill-founded; it is not unusual to note in young students, at the end of their formative years, a sort of con-

[1] This does not detract in the least from the capital importance of the contemplative life properly so-called.

[2] Cardinal Suenens, *op. cit.*, p. 119.

ventional rigidity or torpor. It is worth while to consider this matter and seek some way of establishing a balanced programme, in which all the elements of training will be harmonized.[1]

One major superior writes along the same lines: 'The sisters are called to live their Christian life and their vows in the context of an apostolate in the midst of the world; is it normal that they be completely cut off from this environment and from any contact with parish life during all their time of formation?'

Habits formed during the noviceship are generally very difficult to change. The same superior continues:

The sisters live *on the fringe* of the world they are called to evangelize; they do not become a part of it. Nevertheless and without suspecting it, they are gradually influenced by the materialism of the world. How can they train young people and arouse enthusiasm for the apostolic evangelization of a world from which they are separated by their way of life? Besides, there is a very great difference between their vision of the world they left ten, twenty, or thirty years ago, and the world of today. The life of active religious is not adapted to the needs of the present; perhaps this is because it was not thought out for its own sake, but was excessively modelled on the forms of early monasticism. Active religious communities are encumbered by useless monastic practices such an enclosure which allows no friendly welcome to be given, and arbitrary timetables difficult to adjust to the present requirements of evangelization.[2]

Often young sisters are assigned to apostolic works immediately after the novitiate, without the benefit of prac-

[1] Cardinal Suenens, *op. cit.*, p. 119.
[2] The above letter is quoted literally, in spite of its somewhat radical character.

tical training. Certain Congregations send them out even before the end of the canonical novitiate. But whether before or after profession, young sisters sent out on missions after such a novitiate are exposed to a twofold danger:[1] that of defending at any cost the system of spirituality learned in the noviceship, without infusing into it a new vitality in which apostolic contacts are a help to prayer; and that of abandoning this same system on the plea that it is unsuited to a rhythm of life for which they have not been prepared. One danger is as much to be feared as the other. Cardinal Suenens reminds us that 'the religion of Christ . . . embraces every department of man's life, and claims to penetrate it through and through. One of the chief merits of our age has been to recall that Christ is not alone the life of the soul, but the life of the whole man, and that nothing is independent of his action. . . . To restrict Christianity to a few pious exercises, however important, is to mutilate it.[2] 'There is more than one kind of silence; and we may argue too readily from the silence of a life absorbed in prayer, and take refuge in a silence that is mere emptiness, escapism and a shirking of the active apostolate.'[3]

Evangelization engages the whole person of the apostle in the whole life of those confided to him. Prayer is one form of this engagement and it is, as we have seen, a very exacting form.[4] But prayer could be a refuge or an alibi or even an escape from the difficulties of the apostolate and the resistance of the milieu. Such prayer is obviously no longer the prayer of an apostle. 'To claim exemption from action because of one's devotion to prayer is to misunderstand the

[1] Not to mention their lack of training for the apostolate.
[2] *Op. cit.*, p. 19.
[3] *Ibid.*, p. 49.
[4] Cf. *supra*, Part II, Chap. 2.

place of prayer, which must normally flow into action. To exalt the silent apostolate of example and to declare that prayer alone is sufficient without communal action is cutting down a budding tree before it has flowered.'[1] What we have termed false supernaturalism is a sort of retreat before this commitment of the whole person demanded by the apostolate. We must indeed pray much, and the schedule of spiritual exercises is very important for the religious life, but only as a means. Cardinal Suenens remarks with reason:

> God does not fail men, the source of grace does not run dry. There has never perhaps been so much piety in the Church; Communions have increased by millions since the decrees of St Pius X; numberless crowds flock to places of pilgrimage and to Eucharistic and Marian congresses. And yet the world is moving away from Christianity, as its superficial humanization progresses. There is something out of gear: the current of grace does not succeed in breaking through the obstacles of indifference and materialism that arise on all sides.[2]

The situation might be compared to a car whose engine is excellent and has proved its worth—this is the domain of prayer and grace. The bodywork is intact and imposing—this is the world to be evangelized. Yet the car will not go, or it moves haltingly and too slowly, because the transmission is out of order. The trouble will be eliminated by rectifying the cause, not by making a deeper study of the engine. This is false supernaturalism: giving such importance to prayer which is the major element in evangelization, that we are finally blinded to the urgent requirements of the apostolate.

[1] Cardinal Suenens, *op. cit.*, p. 51.
[2] *Ibid.*, pp. 61-2.

III. THE BARRIER OF INSTITUTIONS

Institutions are necessary. There is practically no evangelization carried out by individuals, apart from an institution. A parish is an institution, and so is a diocese. Catholic Action groups, Sodalities, charitable organizations, are institutions. Religious communities and all Congregations are institutions, as well as boarding schools, hospitals, hostels, etc. And within these institutions, individuals exercise specific functions whose traditions or methods also tend to solidify into regulations. All this is necessary for the apostolate.

When religious have charge of an establishment—hospital, clinic, or boarding school—they exercise their apostolate by means of this institution and within its walls. These works have always borne witness to the charity of the Church wherever a need exists, and they must continue to do so. The Church must be present to every misfortune and every apostolic necessity. But an institution constitutes a closed, homogeneous environment, and in order to endure, it must consent to a certain separation from the milieu in which it is located; exchanges between itself and this milieu are carried out by a sort of osmosis.

A school operated by religious, for example, constitutes a homogeneous environment whose walls are the material element, and the sisters living in community, the formal element. The pupils attending the school live habitually in a human milieu in which the family is the principal element, but which is composed of many other elements of various kinds: friendships, holidays, the cinema, radio, television, etc. In coming to school the children leave this setting and penetrate into an enclosed milieu where the sisters await them. There is a continual exchange between the two milieux, that is, between the institution and the world, through the intermediary of the pupils. It must be remembered that these pupils are precisely the ones whom the religious are to evangelize.

I might have used the example of a hospital or clinic. In this case the patients provide the communication between the two milieux, and again, they are the ones to be evangelized by the sisters of the hospital. There was a time when a child or a patient returning home from an institution found himself in an environment not too different from the one which he left, that is, when the family and other relationships together with cultural mediums, were steeped in faith and Christian vitality.[1]

Today it is no longer so. In going to school a girl leaves a milieu more or less Christian. Even when the family is still faithful to its religious duties, the minds of its members are unconsciously being impregnated with materialistic ideas through radio and television, the press, motion pictures, and conversations that constantly propagate these ideas. A girl spends a much longer time away from school than formerly.[2] Elements outside the home exert a far stronger influence on her mentality than the family milieu itself, and parents experience the 'conflict of generations' much earlier than formerly. When she arrives at school, she penetrates into an atmosphere apparently impervious to the world's din and permeated with the Christian spirit, where there are regular times for prayer; in a word, a milieu totally different from that in which she habitually lives. And when in the evening she leaves the religious environment, she finds again the real

[1] Some will question whether this golden age ever existed. Certain regions have been and perhaps still are Christian lands. This is not the place to define this concept with its various possible nuances.

[2] There are fewer 'boarders' than before and many more non-resident students, and holidays are longer.

atmosphere in which her mind is at ease and in which she will spend the rest of her life. The hours spent at school are simply parentheses in her existence.

During this time, the religious continue to be completely separated from the world in which their students are immersed. Besides, their existence is so filled with obligations necessitated by their work and their religious life that they have neither the time nor the possibility of making themselves accessible to the world, which comes to them only in the person of their pupils, one by one. But they do not go out to the world. Their legitimate separation from the world has become a barrier. No doubt it is a protection, but it is also, in fact, an obstacle to evangelization. Their tendency is to practise the policy of the ostrich: close their eyes, and absorb themselves into a narrow personal sphere.[1] The result is that they tend to work by themselves, apart from the clergy, the parish, and Catholic Action organizations.

The consequences are glaring. Many facts and testimonies prove that the teaching imparted in private and parochial schools does not take sufficiently into account the actual conditions in which young people live, and does not prepare them adequately for them. The sisters, enclosed within their school and overburdened by their work, are not fully aware of these problems and sometimes have no idea of them.

One nun, a kindergarten teacher, said of a group of girls who had attended a training course under her direction: 'These former pupils are fervent and live a very good Christian life. Yet they manifest on such subjects as marriage, social questions, and the use of money, truly materialistic views. The religious education received at school has not succeeded in counteracting the influence of the milieu in which they live.'

[1] Cardinal Suenens, *op. cit.*, p. 13.

The rift between religious and the world, created by the very works to which they are dedicated, exists not only in large institutions like boarding schools and hospitals, but also in small communities devoted to various types of charitable works. One priest remarked concerning sisters dedicated to the care of patients in their own homes: 'They are always rushing, calling on their patients—those who could afford a lay nurse as well as the others. They have no time to listen, to reflect, to inquire into the meaning of their religious life. They bypass the principal work to which they should be devoting themselves, the spreading of the Gospel.'

These reflections on the causes of this apparent failure to evangelize, far from exhausting the subject, have hardly scratched the surface. But perhaps it would be better to concentrate our efforts on a search for the positive means of giving the work of the sisters, the evangelical fruitfulness it was meant to have in the designs of God.

14

Conditions for a True Evangelization

What then is Apollos? What is Paul? Servants through whom you believed, as the Lord assigned to each. I planted, Apollos watered, but God gave the growth. . . . He who plants and he who waters are equal . . . for we are fellow workers for God; you are God's field, God's building.

I Cor. 3:5-9

I. THE CHURCH EVANGELIZES

It would be well at this point to make a very simple theological reflection on who is the agent of evangelization. Too often we are under the impression that evangelization is the work of an individual—a priest in his parish, a religious in her community, or a lay apostle in his milieu. Or perhaps we believe it is the work of an institution—hospital, school, or other organization. Or again, it may be the work of a Congregation.

Evangelization is the work of neither Apollos nor Paul (I Cor. 3:3-9), nor anyone else, person or institution. They are only 'fellow workers for God', 'servants of Christ and stewards of the mysteries of God' (I Cor. 4:1); and the world to be converted is 'God's field, God's building'.

Evangelization is the work of Christ,[1] continually acting in the world through the Church, his bride.[2] The Church alone

---

[1] 'For no other foundation can any one lay than that which is laid, which is Jesus Christ' (I Cor. 3:11).
[2] Eph. 5:25; 2 Cor. 11:2; Apoc. 21:2; 21:9-27.

evangelizes, for Christ lives in her and acts through her. All those who labour in 'God's field' (I Cor. 3:9) which is the world to be won, do it within the Church and according to an explicit mandate received from her. The progress of theology on the nature of the Church has been extraordinary in the past few years. Not only has it inspired the writings of specialists, but it has also directed the activity and nourished the prayer of modern apostles.

This theology has already prompted some religious Congregations to re-examine their relations with the diocesan Churches. But time is passing and this evolution is often a slow-moving process; gradually the need was filled by the increasing success of secular institutes. Even these, however, do not always avail themselves of all the opportunities afforded them by the directives of Pius XII in the apostolic constitution *Provida Mater Ecclesia*[1] and the motu proprio *Primo Feliciter*.[2] Above all, secular institutes of women are often influenced too much by the example of the highly organized Congregations. For this reason, some groups of lay workers stress union with the bishop, even to the point of refusing all other commitments than those which place them entirely at the service of the diocese.

But religious can find the same opportunities in their own constitutions and traditions. They are consecrated, that is, they are brides of Christ. Cardinal Suenens writes:[3]

The alliance with Christ which is at the heart of a sister's

[1] 2 February 1947.

[2] 12 March 1948. Cf. Instruction of the S. Cong. of Rel. *Cum Sanctissimus*, 19 March 1948.

[3] Allocution delivered 13 November 1959, at the Abbey of Mont César, Louvain, to retreat directors of religious sisters (*Revue des Communautés Religieuses*, Feb. 1960). Cf. conference given by Cardinal Suenens at the second general congress of the states of perfection, Rome, December 1957.

religious profession, is at the same time an alliance with the Church. . . . The religious consecration that vows her, body and soul, to Christ, vows her therefore to the Church. . . . Religious life is but the full flowering of her baptismal consecration, the completion of her gift to Christ and to the Church. The religious consecrates herself to the living Christ; she also vows herself to him in the Church. . . .

But that very fact, the apostolate of the religious—we refer only to Congregations destined for an active apostolate[1]—must itself also enter into the perspective of the Church. An active religious has no right to limit her vision to the walls of her school, her foundling home, her hospital or her clinic. It must extend as far as the interests of the Church go. . . .

This universality derives from the fact that her apostolate, as a component part of a whole greater than itself, is integrated at the diocesan level with that of the bishop, and at the universal level with that of the pope, supreme head of the Church. It is through and by means of the bishop that a religious is united to the pope.[2]

Although she is a daughter of a particular Congregation, yet because she is a daughter of the Church it is to serve the Church that she chose this form of religious vocation. . . .

---

[1] The same may be said of contemplative nuns. Their consecration to Christ and to the Church must incite them to pray unceasingly for the needs of the universal Church and those of the diocese in which their monastery is located.

[2] This link with the pope through the intermediary of the bishop exists chiefly *with regard to the apostolate*. In each diocese the bishop is at the head of all apostolic activities, and each apostle—priest, layman, or religious—works in virtue of a mandate received from the bishop. But *with regard to the consecrated life*, a religious depends directly on the pope (can. 499, § 1). No jurist maintains any longer than a religious, even one belonging to a diocesan congregation, is subject to the bishop in virtue of her vow of obedience.

Congregations exist for the service of the Church and differ only in ways and means of serving. Any self-interest would be a denial of the primacy of the whole.

We return, then, to the fundamental principle: it is not an individual—priest, layman, or religious—who evangelizes; it is the Church alone. In a determinate location, the Church is represented by the bishop, and those who work in the diocese do so under the authority and the responsibility of the bishop. If religious are fully convinced of this fact, they will frequently find in it an occasion of renouncing a personal point of view concerning the interests of their work and of the Congregation; but they will also find therein a source of sound spirituality and of a mystical life springing directly out of the nature of their consecration. Besides, many Congregations are manifesting a desire to labour together under the direction of the bishops.

The Church must, then, be authentically represented in a given milieu or within an institution, if the work of evangelization is to be effectively carried on there. In a parish, for example, the Church is not represented by the clergy alone, as certain parish priests believe; nor by clergy and militant laymen, as some curates would have it; nor again by clergy and sisters, as the latter would sometimes desire.

The Church is represented by a team (to use a modern term) organized under the leadership of the clergy with the collaboration of religious and lay workers. Where this teamwork is operative, there the Church is present and fully active. Where it does not exist or its work is hampered, the Church is not or not sufficiently present, and she does not evangelize. The team is the unique means by which the Church can do her work within the boundaries of a parish.

In a private school, to take another example, the Church is not fully represented by the sisters alone, even acting in close union with one another and in accordance with the directives of their superiors. The Church is represented by a team in which, under the direction of priests appointed by the bishop,[1] the religious of the institution and militant workers chosen from among lay collaborators and from the students (and the students' parents!), work together to evangelize the milieu. If this team is genuinely constituted, it will evangelize in virtue of the dynamism proper to the Church.

Examples could be multiplied and they would all lead to the same conclusion : the Church is present and active when it is represented by a priest, a religious, and a militant layman. Where this collaboration does not exist, there are only free lance workers whose activity is certainly not negligible, but with whom the Church is only indirectly involved when it is not compromised.

Where the team really exists and the leader is conscious of the extent (and limitations) of his role, then the members must learn to work together; and for this purpose they must be given the same formation. It is impossible to go into detail here, because of the great variety of teams. It is not only a question of using the same apostolic methods; all the team members must make a study of the milieu to which they belong and which has been confided to them by the bishop. They must actually assume responsibility for the persons that constitute it.

Finally, the character of such teams demands that the

---

[1] The chaplain of an institution directed by religious should therefore have his rightful place in the team whose work is to evangelize. This implies that the priest is willing to remain within his role without interfering in the direction of the establishment. It also implies that the dioceses, with paternal care, will not only appoint qualified priests to this important ministry, but will also give them the consideration they deserve and which they need in order to fulfil their functions adequately.

bishops and the superiors general of Congregations[1] come to a mutual agreement, so that the transfer of personnel which often takes place in the summer, may not overthrow an edifice laboriously erected. Up to the present, changes have been dictated by the interests of the Congregation; now the horizon must be enlarged. Many dioceses are going out of their way to integrate religious into a joint pastoral effort; such good will must not be discouraged. Wholesale changes which would seriously impede apostolic organizations already set up must be avoided.

Some will perhaps object that it is surely utopian to claim that such apostolic organization is possible everywhere. I should like to answer their objections by citing several examples realized through the initiative of local superiors, or of priests supported by the religious.

1. *At the parish level*

We know of several parishes in which the clergy (pastor and curates), the religious (parochial school teachers and nursing sisters), and militant laymen from the various Catholic Action groups, have formed the habit of meeting together at regular intervals to co-ordinate their apostolic endeavours in the parish.

Here are two concrete cases in which the team was set up through the initiative of the religious themselves. In northern France, in a town composed of many small neighbourhoods, a nursing sister, acting in collaboration with a militant Catholic working-man and his family, organized a pilgrimage to Lourdes for a few families living in one of the neighbourhoods. At this stage there was no question of bringing a priest into the project. These families would be assisted by a Catholic aid society, and would avail themselves of the

[1] Through the intermediary of the diocesan director of religious, where he exists; for not every diocese has one.

hospitality of the Cité Saint-Pierre at Lourdes. Two weeks previous to the date of the pilgrimage, one of the drivers of the society came to map out the itinerary for the twenty people assembled in the lay worker's home, as well as to explain the functioning of the Cité Saint-Pierre (many of the pilgrims had practically never left their native town). At the end of the meeting, in an atmosphere of friendliness, the priest-director of the pilgrimage came to explain what happened at Lourdes over a hundred years ago. The pilgrimage took place in an excellent atmosphere.

After their return, the pilgrims continued to frequent one another's homes, and began to be aware of one another's needs. Before long the lay apostle was able to invite the curate of the parish, who eventually gained access to all the homes of the neighbourhood. The apostolic team was formed with priest, lay workers, and religious.

In another town, open-air centres were created to gather together by zone and by age the children of various parishes. One of these centres was reserved for little boys between six to eight. The curate in charge of this group obtained from a neighbouring motherhouse the collaboration of seven second-year novices.[1] A young married couple helped out by sacrificing two weeks' holiday with pay; several Catholic Action mothers and a few students likewise contributed their services. The apostolic team was set up: priest, religious, laymen. The field of evangelization was clearly defined: not only the little boys themselves, but also their families. The results were very favourable and the fruits of these efforts are still being gathered. The parish barrier has vanished. Both priests and laymen have found out by experience that collaboration with the religious is both possible and valuable. The young religious have had their apostolic sense awakened

[1] That is, novices who have completed their canonical noviceship.

even in the novitiate, and one of them declared that this work had required of her a veritable conversion. The unity of the apostolic team during the vacation period has become a permanent inspiration for the children and their parents. All the parents were visited by the young religious, and all were open to suggestion concerning the educational problems of their children. Among these parents, future lay apostles were discovered. The centre issued a weekly bulletin which became a link between the apostolic team and the parents. Finally, in the whole area concerned, all the priests of the parishes and all Catholic Action workers were kept informed of the work accomplished.

2. *At the level of institutions directed by religious*

Included under this heading are hospitals, clinics, orphanages, girls' hostels, boarding schools, etc. In each case there is a milieu to evangelize: patients, girls, or children, not forgetting the lay collaborators of the religious. Finally, there are the families of all these people.

In every institution of this kind a typical apostolic team should be set up. At its head will be the priest appointed by the bishop—probably the chaplain; where this is not possible, the bishop would appoint another priest. The place of the religious in the team is, of course, of capital importance. But they should be accompanied by lay apostles recruited from the milieu which they are to evangelize—nurses or other hospital personnel, children, or even the relatives of either.

Let it not be said that this is impossible. Pope Pius XII has written:

The most substantial and widespread help given to Catholic Action will doubtless come . . . from the numerous religious orders. . . . They will be especially helpful by preparing for Catholic Action from the earliest years, the children whom they are educating in the schools and colleges directed by religious institutes. They must begin by drawing young people to the practice of the apostolate, then exhort them with care and perseverance to join the organizations of Catholic Action. If these are lacking, let the religious themselves set them up. One can say that there is no better time than schooldays and no place more favourable than school and college to train young people in Catholic Action.[1]

As Cardinal Suenens accurately remarks: 'In every Christian resides a force that asks to be set at work. It is the task of that special élite, the religious—*illustrior portio gregis Christi* —to find out and train these helpers of God, in order that Christ may through them give himself in full measure to the world.'[2]

In one academy for girls, the regional apostolate was organized as follows. A committee was created composed of the priest, a religious, a lay teacher and an elected student from each class. Now the solution of concrete problems is entrusted to the apostolic committee; for example, the preparation of a truly Christian Christmas gathering in counteraction to a prevalent pagan mentality; plans for Holy Week; the problem of prayer, etc. Students are invited to co-operate with the committee by means of a suggestion box. The group acts rather by a kind of osmosis than by public communications.

Another example is significant in that it illustrates to what extent religious educators can be imbued with profound concern for the apostolate.

At a meeting of a group of persons devoted to the aposto-

[1] *Acta Apostolicae Sedis*, Vol. XXVIII, No. 5, p. 159.
The Lay Apostolate, Papal Teachings (Boston: St Paul Editions, 1961), pp. 371-2.
[2] *Op Cit.*, p. 104.

late among the working classes, a religious brother, principal of one of the city schools, was explaining the function of religious teachers in the apostolic organization. They had first, he said, taken an inventory of the number of their pupils and the status of their parents. Out of 1,640 pupils, 1,154 (70 per cent) were children of working-men and employees. The brother continued:

> We investigated the actual situation in which our pupils live. The school is an artificial and homogeneous milieu, while the children's lives are conditioned by the social status of their parents, the housing situation, and the neighbourhood. Are the parents business men, textile or metal workers, builders? Do they work for a company, on call, or on a straight salary basis? Do they work overtime? Are they unemployed? Do they live in slums, housing developments, or residential areas? Do the children play in a yard or garden, or on the streets and public squares? . . . How are they influenced by their parents' culture or lack of it, by their opinions, their leisure time occupations?
>
> The apostolate to the working classes has made us aware that as Christian educators, we must take all these elements into consideration.
>
> At the present time it is impossible to content ourselves with the presentation of an idealized Christian life, without taking account of these realities. Where would our pupils find the solution to the difficulties they experience in the midst of adults whose life contradicts our teaching?
>
> We cannot teach them as if they lived in a truly Christian family. Our task is to show them how to discover true values, at once human and Christian—charity, justice, uprightness, team-work, etc.
>
> We tried to find out by means of a questionnaire, whether our curriculum fostered the development of these values.
>
> Events in the daily life of our children affect their life of faith. To observe these events and take them into

account is a first step in our teaching. To see God in them in order to be true Christian educators is surely the second.

Our desire is to collaborate with everyone towards a more human and more Christian education of the children.

Since we cannot be present at every phase of the children's lives, we must establish contacts with all those who are in a position to help us—parents, lay apostles, educators in every field. . . . The school . . . is also the concern of the parents of former pupils who are now on their own, and of all Christians, even those who have no children in school. Some parents entrust their children to the parochial school for the sole reason that they seem to get better teaching there. We have contacts with these persons whose relations with the Church are practically non-existent. The educational problems of their children may afford us the opportunity of establishing a relationship between them and the lay workers.

We are happy to be able to enter into the apostolate for working people, for we are thus integrated with the apostolate of the Church.

To this report read by the brother principal in the name of all the religious educators of the region, the superior, as representing the girls' schools, was invited to add a comment if she so desired. She said:

We should be all the more alert to these problems because we are entrusted with the children's formation from their earliest years. . . . A new course has been implemented for girls who do not have the intellectual ability to prepare for an academic examination. They make a special study of their milieu. They take all their subjects, even mathematics, from the point of view of this study; and I have noticed that this year, they seem to enjoy their work. They are intensely interested in this type of teaching. We also wish to prepare them for the Y.C.W. These girls who do not take examinations are future young Catholic workers, and they must be prepared for this.

One of the priests who directed the meeting drew the following conclusion:

> In this co-ordinated effort of priests, religious, and active laymen, we study together the mentality of a neighbourhood, to find out what may constitute an obstacle to the faith there. We try to understand it, for we are somewhat separated from this life. Unless we work together, we cannot evangelize.

This testimony has been quoted at length, not only because of its recent date, but also because it demonstrates how the necessity of evangelizing a world bent on materialism, brings together priests, religious and laymen in a concrete attempt to unite their efforts in apostolic team-work. Certainly this is not the only example; everywhere the same need is leading to the same effort. These examples have been cited for the encouragement which other priests and religious may find therein, to create in that section of 'God's field' confided to them, a similar team.

II. REFORM OR ADAPTATION

These two words do not have the same meaning. Reform signifies a certain break with the past with a somewhat stronger implications. Adaptation, on the other hand, is a word very frequently used by the Sovereign Pontiff, and the Sacred Congregation of Religious places the emphasis on continuity.[1] Many religious Congregations have already fol-

[1] Cf. Pius XII, Discourse to the General Congregation of the Society of Jesus, 17 September 1946; Letter to Cardinal Micara on the occasion of the first international congress of religious, 12 November 1950; Apostolic Constitution (*Sponsa Christi*, 21 November 1950; Discourse to members of the second congress of states of perfection, 9 December 1957; Discourse of Rev. Fr Larraona at the same congress (Courtois, *States of Perfection*). Some of these texts may be found in Part I, Chapter 2.

lowed to the letter these formal instructions of the Church. Supported by their example, I should like to help other Congregations to evolve, to modify their concept of the apostolate and their methods of forming young religious, in order to bring about true evangelization.

1. *Adaptation of the apostolic life*

(a) The fundamental principle is this: beyond traditions and even the constitutions, the important thing is accurately to determine *the apostolic intuition of the founder*.[1]

In November 1959, Cardinal Alfrinks, Archbishop of Utrecht, before an audience of several hundred general and local superiors of his diocese, gave a momentous conference; I give here the translation of some of the important parts.[2]

Each Order or Congregation sprang out of a determinate need or difficulty of the Church at the time, either a religious difficulty, or a social difficulty with repercussions in the distress of souls. Today, when the need for a Christian presence in a dechristianized world is becoming acute, secular institutes are springing up everywhere in order to adapt ancient forms of the religious life to the spiritual distress of a world without God. The service of the Church, as well as the service of man, is the foundation of the religious state. . . .

But times change, and with them, the needs of the Church. What, at a given period, was a charitable service of extreme importance, may at another period become less urgent, perhaps even superfluous, perhaps even insignificant. . . . When needs change, then we must take a different direction. The Church always has distress to alleviate, and to whom will she turn, if not to the wealth of religious Congregations within her fold? They must not fear becoming unfaithful to the spirit of the founder and

[1] Cf. Part I, Chapter 2.
[2] *Katholiek Archief*, No. 46, 14th year, 11 December 1959.

the proper character of the Congregation. Otherwise they would fall into the error of preferring the particular spirit of the Congregation to the essential character of the religious state, namely the service of the Church. Were the founders alive today, they would not be so narrow as to hold to something which is over and done with. Their foundation sprang precisely out of the need of the period. Each period has its needs and the Church expects religious institutes, while holding to what is essential in their spirit, to show a suppleness of adaptation to needs which change with the times. The reason of their existence is not the preservation of something, but above all the service of the Church.

For example, teaching and nursing are not undertaken for the purpose of relieving pressing difficulties today as they were formerly. In the days when most of your Congregations were founded, these were true works of charity in that they were, first, exercised by religious for the love of neighbour; and secondly, they were done gratuitously or for a very small remuneration.

Today it is no longer so. No doubt a religious as such can still devote herself to these tasks for love of the neighbour. But these are now salaried occupations considered as professions rather than vocations, and as such are no longer an institutional manifestation of Christian charity.

Although they may demand much love, teaching, and to a certain extent the care of the sick, they are no longer institutionally and necessarily linked with Christian charity, except in certain accidental circumstances in which more than ordinary self-sacrifice and normal devotedness are required

I do not imply that these professions can be handled as easily by laymen as by religious. In fact, I hope that teaching and nursing, as exercised by religious, will always have a distinctive character not present in the same works carried out by laymen. But here I refer to something else.

I refer to the fact that certain tasks of Christian service should be performed by lay persons, thus freeing religious

for forms of charity not so easily undertaken by laymen.
. . . Thus religious will be freed for other works of the
Church.

For religious to replace laymen, for example, in schools
for privileged children, is contrary to common sense. If a
Congregation devotes itself to the ministry of charity in
the form of teaching, it should seek to exercise this charity
in educating children who are underprivileged spiritually
or socially, rather than for interested considerations.

And if it seeks in the field of nursing objectives more
eloquently indicative of charity than those incidental to
a normal hospital routine, there is the care of the chronic-
ally ill, the aged, the abandoned, and especially the feeble-
minded—all these are areas in which there exists a
deficiency which reflects no credit upon our Catholic
milieu. . . .[1]

There should never be any rivalry between lay persons
and religious in the service of the Church—there is room
for both. But religious should occupy the positions that
require a greater amount of self-sacrifice and engage the
whole person. It is thus we can reach present distressing
situations in the Church. There is, for example, social work
in the slums, among the under-privileged.

In order to bring this about, some modifications will obviously be needed in the programme of the works of the
institute. This may present difficulties, but not, it would
seem, major obstacles.

Two important concerns must be kept in mind:

1. It is not a question of a few external changes such as
adopting a new habit or discarding the old coif, desirable
as this may be. Still less is there question of granting more
freedom by suppressing certain usages. There is question
of a new spirit, of becoming alive to the present-day needs
of the Church. This new spirit is none other than the spirit
which saw the birth of the Congregation: the spirit of
Christian charity eager to devote itself to the needs of its

[1] In the Netherlands.

time. Christian charity may manifest itself in new ways; but if it is not vivified by this changeless spirit, it will serve no good purpose either for the religious themselves, or for the Church.

2. The second concern is the following. This new spirit must always be referred to as the essential character of the religious state. . . . We have chosen the state of virginity for the service of the Church. Since this service today requires the religious to work outside her convent much more than formerly, care must be be taken to give her a much stronger religious formation than before.

These modern times demand much of you: a continual adaptation, a great suppleness of mind. Each new postulant brings with her many more problems than previously. Welcome her with an open heart. Each one needs much more attention and understanding on the part of the superior than formerly. You cannot mould them all into uniform models. . . .

Another voice echoes that of Cardinal Alfrinks; the voice of Cardinal Suenens, from Belgium:

To love Christ is to love, not an abstract Christ, but Christ living in the Church of our time. This truth is important for it counteracts any anachronism and clarifies the urgent need to keep abreast of the Church and the world of today. It is in the Church of today that the Holy Spirit operates. . . .

Consequently, the means of being faithful to the spirit of the founders, who themselves entered fully into the ecclesial grace proper to their time, is to enter into the ecclesial grace proper to our own. It is the founder himself who insistently invites you to express the love of Christ which inspired his own foundation, in a vital, present-day, modernized translation—not primarily from a desire to be modern, but through fidelity to the grace of God given to the Church of our day.[1]

[1] Allocution delivered 13 November 1959, to retreat directors of religious sisters.

It is to be noted that these authoritative voices insist on the essential fact that adaptation to the present needs of the Church is the only way to be truly faithful to the spirit of the founder, and that this loyalty is, in reality, loyalty to the Church.

(b) What, then, will be *the hierarchy of works* proper to the religious of today? We cannot enter into detail; each Congregation must make its own examination of conscience. We shall merely outline a few principles.

Teaching remains a work of capital importance in the Church. The Sovereign Pontiff and the hierarchy have insisted on the right of the Church and the duty of Christians to have their proper system of education in which not only are state requirements complied with, but children are given a Christian vision of the world and a true religious formation. Thus teaching has value in the eyes of the Church only in the measure that it constitutes a total education of the baptized person in view of the christianization of the world. If, in schools and academies operated by religious, the evangelization of the students is not the primary concern, these religious are not accomplishing the work entrusted to them by the Church today.

Within this work of education, certain sectors remain the exclusive domain of religious, for example, teaching underprivileged and subnormal children.

In the field of nursing, religious should not surrender entirely to lay persons all direct contact with the patients. In this service of the Lord in the person of his suffering members they must desire to evangelize the sick, tactfully indeed, but with the will to prepare them not only for death, but to return to the life of the world. For this purpose they must work in union with the chaplain and lay apostles, and in collaboration with the parish clergy.

Girls' hostels have value in the Church of today only if a work of true evangelization is carried on there. 'Too many religious spend their life in purely material work, more or less as innkeepers, exerting no influence on the persons residing in their houses.'[1]

In all these works, lay collaborators must be used whenever possible. 'An effort will be made . . . wherever possible, and even at the cost of a financial sacrifice, to entrust certain duties or classes in the institution to lay people, so that the nuns may be set free to make sure of the all-important mission of training the laity.'[2] I am acquainted with superiors of nursing sisters, who employ many lay nurses in order that the sisters may be better able to do the work of evangelization. This implies that they must become able to train auxiliary helpers both spiritually and professionally. The urgent need of evangelizing does not limit the field of action to the word of God alone. In a community, some must be able to excel in certain fields of human activity. But these must be the positions that require true competence, not those which could be filled by anybody. In every sector of activity, whether spiritual or temporal, the posts filled by the religious must be those requiring true qualities of leadership and formative influence.

This implies on the part of communities the willingness to make financial sacrifices for the training of the religious, sometimes very burdensome ones. But they will find therein a poverty adapted to the needs of our time, and the occasion of abandoning themselves in faith to the fatherly Providence of God.

Finally, a rigorous hierarchy must be established in the tasks performed by religious within a given house. Those

[1] Cardinal Suenens, *ibid.*
[2] Cardinal Suenens, *The Gospel to Every Creature*, p. 91.

which have value, either directly or indirectly, for the work of evangelization must be kept; all the others must be eliminated. In our day it is scandalous to tolerate that religious spend their Sunday afternoons totalling the church collections, or that they have charge of the parish church or hall. They did not consecrate themselves to God to become domestics of the clergy.

2. *Adaptation the religious formation in view of evangelization*

(a) *An active postulancy*

In Congregations of religious who make perpetual vows, Canon Law requires only that the postulancy last six entire months (Canon 539, § 1). It should be made in the novitiate house, but may also be made in another house of the Congregation, provided the constitutions are faithfully observed there and that an exemplary religious has charge of the postulants (Canon 540, § 1). Their dress is to be modest, and different from that of the novices (Canon 540, § 2).

These prescriptions are very wise and very broad, and therefore leave us free to propose a new manner of conceiving the postulancy.

In principle, it should be a time of transition permitting superiors to weigh a vocation, and subjects to judge whether they are suited to continue in the way they selected at the outset.

In actual fact things happen quite otherwise. The break with the world is made at the beginning of the postulancy, which is thus nothing less than a noviceship begun six months early. It is not easy for a girl to return home after entering the convent, for she has definitely said good-bye to family and friends before leaving, and has been formally received into the convent. So frequently a girl who leaves the postulancy after a few months on realizing this is not her vocation, is marked perhaps for life on account of the formality with which she abandoned the world in the first place. So many others who never dared return to the world bear painfully the burden of a life not meant for them, and finally they also withdraw, sometimes after many years.

It would seem more logical for girls who think they might have a vocation, tentatively to fulfil the canonical postulancy without committing themselves for the future. It is not unusual today for girls to leave their family and milieu for purposes of study. An absence of six months would hardly appear extraordinary.

The postulants would live the life of the other sisters, in the novitiate house for a time, then in one or several missions of the institute, where they would become acquainted with their future religious life and the forms of apostolate to which they will dedicate themselves.

After the postulancy they would return to their family for a few days.[1] Then with full knowledge and in complete freedom, they would make up their mind whether or not they wish to commit themselves to the service of the Lord. Only at this point would it become officially known that they are entering the convent; and then the formalities could take place.

(b) *An efficacious noviceship*

The subject of the noviceship has been brought up more than once in the course of this work. It would be desirable not only to prolong it, but also to eliminate the gap that exists between the formation given in the noviceship and that which the sister receives from her superiors during her entire religious life. Thus this period of capital importance in

---

[1] The code requires a retreat of eight days before beginning the noviceship (C. 541). It does not formally require that the postulancy, the retreat, and the noviceship follow one another without interruption.

the education of an active religious will be fully effective in three areas: it will be a stage of profound religious, intellectual, and apostolic formation. Far from constituting three separate domains, these areas are intimately bound up together.

Since the religious-apostolic life must be inspired by theological faith, religious must understand clearly that this faith will be nourished not only by prayer, but also by study and by action. There is real danger for a future active religious in seeking the nourishment of her faith in prayer alone. In order to develop, faith needs to radiate and be exercised in true apostolic activity. To deprive it of every opportunity of giving itself to others is to weaken it and lessen its natural dynamism. This is all the more important today, when many candidates discover the value of religious consecration through their Catholic Action apostolate.

A religious formation founded on prayer and recollection alone is to be avoided. It is true that the canonical year of noviceship should be characterized by definite separation from the world. But this school of prayer founded on silence, meditation on the Bible, and a study of the masters of the spiritual life, should be followed in the second year by a prudent initiation into the apostolate, the beginning of a lifetime formation in which prayer and apostolic action mutually enrich each other.

This formation begun in the noviceship should be continued several years after profession, and in the same spirit. For it must enable the religious to integrate into one movement her prayer life, the total Christian mystery, and an openness to the realities of daily life.

(c) *Formation of the religious to her apostolic mission by reflection on the apostolate in community*

In the second part of this work, much stress was laid on

the necessity of developing the spiritual life of the sisters, not only during the noviceship, but in the whole course of their life. For this purpose superiors are needed who will be true educators. The same must be said concerning apostolic formation, which must be given not only during the years of study, but throughout life, and for this superiors must be prepared. But there exists an important difference between spiritual and apostolic formation; the first is an individual work, but the second can only be given in community. It has been stated repeatedly that an isolated religious cannot evangelize; it is the community that evangelizes, in the measure in which it presents an authentic image of the Church. Apostolic formation is therefore given in and by the community, and the most efficacious means is *apostolic reflection in common.*

The matter for this reflection is to be found in daily life, that is, in the facts observed and the conversations heard in the course of the sisters' daily occupations. They must take care not to limit themselves to the convenient ground of general theories, nor to deviate into a sort of public examination of conscience. Concrete facts disclose living persons whom they must consider with love, without tolerating in themselves that mental block erected by judgements based on principles.

It is not a question of finding solutions or of determining practical common attitudes. It is much more than that.

> Our own mentality must be profoundly transformed. We must see persons as Christ sees them; we must hear him calling them. . . . Our renewal of life will make us conscious that God is at work in the world, in persons and events. . . .
> Apostolic reflection in community must develop a mis-

sionary spirit in us by enabling us to discover more and more, the immense spiritual destitution of men. . . . We must look at the world with eyes of faith, in order to be able to make the prayer of praise to God.[1]

For this communal apostolic reflection to be possible, a determinate time must be assigned to it in the weekly schedule, apart from meals and recreations; a period long enough to allow for psychological delays.

This period of communal reflection should, moreover, accord with a total missionary outlook in the community, and with a habit of communal thinking and group activity. Thus will be realized, once again, the capital importance of the superior.

Just as times of prayer are moments of concentrated strength in a day that should be a continual prayer, so this communal apostolic revision is a moment of strength in a community life that is unceasingly apostolic. Thus each sister will gradually become educated for her mission of evangelization, by regular reflection with her sisters on the concrete facts of the apostolate and the unceasing calls of God through the events of life.

(d) *A prudent openness of the community to the outside world*

The world to be evangelized is becoming increasingly materialistic. It is therefore advisable that active religious make contact with this world without being hampered by regulations inherited from mediaeval monasteries and strongly affected by a discipline of strict enclosure. The solution does not lie in first seeking artificial means of contact with the exterior. Before all we must be deeply convinced of

[1] M. le Vicaire Général Fauchet, Conference given at the regional congresses of religious devoted to nursing and social service, Lille and Tolouse, 1959.

this truth, that evangelization demands a certain connaturality with the area to be evangelized.

It is because religious try to live apart from the world that the lay apostolate is being organized without them, except for a few youth groups. The laws of common enclosure must indeed be observed, but the Code of Canon Law forbids only the admission of persons of the other sex (Canon 604, § 1).

I am acquainted with religious who welcome to their table girls passing through their locality. Is this a revolution? Perhaps some will have none of it, protesting that there is risk of abuse.[1] There can never be any education without risks. It is all the more reason why religious should be given a formation in depth. An enlightened conscience is a better guide than a conscience imprisoned in regulations that will not permit human contacts necessary for any evangelization.

Along the same line it is recommended that certain Congregations open their doors to girls wishing to make a retreat. True, retreat houses do exist; but retreatants' quarters are removed from the convent and the retreatants have no contact with the religious life. If, on the contrary, these girls or women were admitted to a measure of community life—at least to meals and the divine Office—it would be a powerful means of sanctification for them, while it would demand of the religious that their life be authentic.

Evangelization demands, in summary, that the apostle unceasingly should have access to two realities: supernatural realities, by an ever increasing theological life; and human realities, by a genuine esteem for them and a great openness of mind. For him, these are the two sources at which his soul is renewed.

[1] Would this be the reason why certain Congregations will not admit to their table religious of other Congregations passing through the city?

He must therefore take care never to cut himself off from them. It would indeed be unfortunate to allow his soul to be suffocated through lack of prayer. It would be equally unfortunate for him to lose contact with human realities by tolerating obsolete customs, pointless traditions, and habits that are out of date.

The past, by its own right, can never merit our loyalty; only the Church commands it.

Conclusion

ON REACHING the close of this work, I am fully aware that it is both incomplete and transitory; in fact, I cherish the hope that it will quickly be outmoded and overtaken.

The work is *incomplete* for several reasons. First, the human reality with which it deals is immense and extremely diversified. How is it possible to address more than five hundred French Congregations at once, not to mention the many others who have approximately the same problems? How, in a limited number of pages, make enough distinctions not to leave an impression of misinterpretation and misunderstanding?

Moreover, the problems posed—religious formation, and adaptation to the apostolate of the Church—are many and complex. Each would require a volume in which to be treated adequately.

It was impossible to cover these subjects exhaustively, nor did I attempt to do so. My intention was rather to show the link that unites them. In a word, I set out to make a study of the very existence of an active religious. Its external aspects were the most obvious: devotedness even to overwork, and problems occasioned by increasingly close contacts with a technological and dechristianized civilization.

Part two raised the question of the profound spiritual formation demanded by these new problems. The training given during the novitiate is no longer sufficient. A sister's formation should continue for the rest of her religious life. Three examples were selected, three areas in which such a formation could be given: prayer, fraternal charity, and an understanding of suffering. In order that such an education might be successful, the third part of this book outlined a programme for the guidance of superiors.

Finally, part four inquired how the immense reserves of devotedness accumulated by the sisters could be channelled, renewed, and adapted to the needs of today's Church, in genuine loyalty to the apostolic intuition of the founders.

In brief, this work is an attempt to answer the questions raised by the present situation of religious Congregations.

It is for this reason that I hope that the book will quickly be *outmoded* and *surpassed*. This is not intended as a paradox. The Church is constantly evolving; this is why she is always young. It is the institutions that grow old and fossilized in 'traditions' that claim to represent genuine 'tradition'. Religious Congregations do not escape this danger. But we who know them well can bear witness to this: there is no sector of the Church in which there exists more good will, more openness to reality, and a greater desire to adapt, than in religious Congregations. True, they do not all advance with equal alacrity. Those who seem unable to get out of their routine have already doomed themselves to extinction. But new Congregations are springing up, along with the secular institutes, and this too is a manifestation of the Church's eternal youth.

Some Congregations have already found their own personal answer to the questions posed in this book, and their example has helped to crystallize the thoughts outlined here. Other Congregations have undertaken a fundamental reform of their methods of spiritual formation and apostolic activity.

There is reason to believe that, within ten years, this renovation will be complete everywhere. If this hope is justified, the present work will then be surpassed by the actual reality.

But the principles which have inspired it will not be surpassed. A religious institution (of which a Congregation is a typical example) may, at any moment in its history, be obliged to make a choice. Since the world is constantly evolving and new problems must always be met, it is imperative that we have the intelligence and openness of mind to distinguish between accidental traditions and 'tradition'. At every port we must be daring enough to change ships. The only barque we must never leave is that of the Church.